PRAISE FOR **FACING GOLIATH**

Whenever I'm around J. P. Jones, I'm always struck by two traits: faithfulness and consistency. He is faithful in his teaching of truth, faithful to his family, and faithful in building men who can in turn build other men. J. P.'s compass, his true North, is consistently teaching and implementing the truth of Christ. I've been with him and his men on many occasions, and they are attempting to live out the truths in this book. They are just a bunch of broken guys who are facing up to their junk and following the Lord every day. It's called discipleship.

Steve Farrar
Founder and Chairman of Men's Leadership Ministries
Author of *Point Man, Finishing Strong, Battle Ready* and *Real Valor*

In *Facing Goliath*, J. P. Jones writes about the fact that every man slugs it out daily with his enemy in the spiritual battle. I appreciate J. P.'s humor, candor, man-to-man style and biblical advice about winning the fight. *Facing Goliath* will help every man recognize the Goliaths in his path and will give him the tools to be victorious and press on in his pursuit of God. *Facing Goliath* is a biblical message given by a real man!

Jake Ellenberger
UFC Fighter, Top Contender, Welterweight Division

We all will face our Goliaths. My friend J. P. has written a much-needed encouragement and exhortation that you might say is "for men only." J. P. Jones is candid, humorous and, most importantly, draws significant truths straight from Scripture.

Greg Laurie
Evangelist at Harvest Crusades
Senior Pastor of Harvest Christian Fellowship

J. P. is a man's man who writes with keen insight into the world of men. He understands the struggles of leading a business, a church and a home. J. P. writes with firm conviction and biblical truth. The contemporary areas discussed in this book will provide valuable insights into integrating biblical truth with real-life struggles faced by all men. *Facing Goliath* lays out a clear path for a man to defeat his giants and press on toward the goal of knowing Christ.

Dr. Michael Anthony
President of Hume Lake Christian Camp and Ministries
Professor of Christian Education at Biola University and Talbot Seminary
Author of *Moving On, Moving Forward* and *The Effective Church Board: Mentoring and Training Servant Leaders*

J. P. Jones has the rare ability to get inside the mind of men. In *Facing Goliath*, he tackles important issues of a man's life with truth, bluntness (!) and practicality. Few people in the world can communicate as effectively on the tough issues and struggles relating to men as J. P. *Facing Goliath* is a must-read for men who want to win the battles in their lives. There is life-changing wisdom on every page and truth to set men free.

Jim Burns
President of HomeWord
Author of *Creating an Intimate Marriage* and *Confident Parenting*

Facing Goliath is a must-read for every man. It is truly a brilliant piece of work! This book will be my go-to guide for my men's ministry for many years to come. Pastor J. P. has done an outstanding job in treating men's real issues with an amazing synergy of Scriptural depth and real-life stories—something to which every man can relate. This is a compelling read that I have recommended to many colleagues! Finally, an amazing all-around, gospel-centered tool for every man!

Andrea Giorgi
Senior Pastor, Chiesa Evangelica Logos Church, Florence, Italy
Director of the Logos Theological Academy
Country Director for Agape Italia (Campus Crusade for Christ International)

I love the story of David and Goliath and how it parallels the life of a man of God today! God is calling men to step up and not only lead their families but also their churches, their workplaces, and wherever God has them. I particularly love the story of when David ran to the battlefield because he knew he would find God there. Through David's talents, gifts and abilities, he was created to serve God and defeat the giant that was in his life. *Facing Goliath* is a reminder to men to give their battles to the Lord. I would challenge any man of God to read this book and defeat the giants that are in his life!

Mark Munoz
Two-time All American Wrestler from Oklahoma State University
UFC Fighter, Ranked #5 in the World of Mixed Martial Arts

J. P. has crafted a book that calls men to face the Goliaths in their lives, whether that is doubt, fear, lust or anger . . . and as he writes, the gospel is unveiled. With discussion questions at the end of each chapter, *Facing Goliath* is a tremendous study for all men's groups and for individuals, wherever they are at in their spiritual journey. I will use this book time and time again in the years to come.

Dave Burns
Director of Adult Ministries, Mount Hermon Conference Center

Few men I have had the privilege of knowing have "run to the battle" with the ferocity of J. P. Jones. His real strength is not a result of his time in the gym, but is derived from his deep affection for and allegiance to Jesus Christ. For more than 30 years, I have watched him run to the battle as a great father, husband, missionary, pastor and church planter. But I've also watched him run to the battle when little seemed clear and when dreams appeared to be dashed on the rocks. When his Goliath looked huge, he picked up stones to face it. *Facing Goliath* is a book for every man, written by a man who's lived it. Read it, and then choose your stones.

Steve Osborn
Men's Pastor at the Evangelical Free Church of Fullerton, California
Adjunct Professor for Biblical Studies at Biola University

Facing Goliath is a tactical operations manual for the spiritual battles we are subjected to as men. The enemy is a master of asymmetric warfare. We are at *war*—and the devil does not fight fair. J. P.'s revelation and application of the power of the gospel can help us overcome the giants we face—giants that reveal themselves in a variety of forms. J. P. exposes them and provides a means of employing the appropriate tactics that can lead to victory. It is time we honor the words of our Savior, put on our battle armor, and run to the fight!

Lieutenant Jason Park
Orange County Sheriff's Department, SWAT Team

Facing Goliath is real and relevant. J. P. Jones understands men and the world in which we live. He provides biblical solutions to common challenges. Every man needs to read and apply this book.

Steve Reynolds
Pastor and Author of *Bod4God* and *Get Off the Couch*

War heroes are memorialized in statues and named in parkways, and their stories are retold in textbooks and chronicled in movies. Men were made to be heroes, but no one falls into victory—it takes a leap of faith. In *Facing Goliath*, J. P. Jones challenges men to take that leap with their eyes wide open. Every man will face his battles, and most will retreat from the front rather than learn the strategies given by God to win. Don't concede defeat—use the insights found in this book to become the hero God made you to be! I recommend *Facing Goliath* to any man who aspires to victorious living.

Bob Shank
Founder/CEO of The Master's Program
Author of *LifeMastery*

Finally—a book on biblical truth written with testosterone! Set against the backdrop of David's heroic first-round knockout of Goliath, men can now see it for what it really was: not merely a man battling a giant, but a man full of faith battling the biggest, baddest obstacle of his era. Smartly, and with Y-chromosome, J. P. carries us into the same battle-field, arming us with a time-honored battle plan and foxhole adjustments to take down the biggest giants of our era. All the time, he reminds us that "the battle is the Lord's."

Ron Walters
Senior Vice President, Ministry Relations for Salem Communications

A book is as good as its author. In the 30-plus years I have known J. P. Jones, my best and closest friend, I can honestly say that what he has to offer comes from the depth of his character before the Lord. This talk about fighting the spiritual battle and winning it has been brewing in his life for years. He's lived it, taught it and knows it. Now we all get to read of his richest discoveries about walking victoriously with the Christ.

Todd Wendorff
Senior Pastor, River Community Church
Author of the *Life Together* series and *Every Man Series*

**HOW A MAN
OVERCOMES HIS GIANTS
TO FOLLOW CHRIST**

J. P. JONES

FACING

BakerBooks

a division of Baker Publishing Group
Grand Rapids, Michigan

© 2013 by J. P. Jones

Published by Baker Books
a division of Baker Publishing Group
P.O. Box 6287, Grand Rapids, MI 49516-6287
www.bakerbooks.com

Baker Books edition published 2014
ISBN 978-0-8010-1775-9

Previously published by Regal Books

Printed in the United States of America

The Library of Congress has cataloged the original edition as follows:
  Jones, J. P. (John Paul), 1955-
    Facing Goliath : how a man overcomes his giants to follow Christ / J.P. Jones.
      pages cm.
    Includes bibliographical references and index.
    ISBN 978-0-8307-6633-8 (pbk.)
    1. Christian men—Religious life. I. Title.
  BV4528.2.J655 2013
  248.8'42—dc23   2013008298

15   16   17   18   19   20   7   6   5   4   3   2

I dedicate this book to my wife and children.

*Donna, you are God's gift to me and the love of my life.
May the Lord give you your holiest desires.*

*Taylor, you are a warrior for Christ.
May God make you brave, strong and courageous.*

*Kylie, you are my precious daughter.
May you always shine with God's love.*

*Ashton, you are my baby.
May you fear the Lord and always walk in His love.*

CONTENTS

WHEN DESIRE AND DISCIPLINE ARE NOT ENOUGH

BY KENNY LUCK

Let's face it: *repeated failures will depress us.* Not achieving much-needed breakthroughs or visible changes in our personal lives will sap our energy and begin to color our world with shades of finality and fatality.

We call the issues, people, character flaws or demons we can't defeat "problems" or "obstacles." My spiritual mentor, J. P. Jones, calls them "Goliaths." Whatever form our Goliaths take, they are imposing to face, their continued presence in our lives mocks us repeatedly, and the idea of ever slaying, overcoming or defeating them is daunting.

Permitting a Goliath to exist in your life on a consistent basis will produce self-loathing and destroy your relationships with God and people. Just the way the devil likes it. But even more sinister and damaging is that your thinking about God will become limited, polluted and cynical. I know this from personal experience.

Goliaths will keep us from realizing the promise of a powerful life in God and the fullness that Jesus promised (see John 10:10). As followers of Christ, we know that no issue, man, defect of character or circumstance can have that right or go unchallenged. Courage is needed, and we must start by walking toward the enemy.

In *Facing Goliath,* J. P. will arm you with truths that will sink deep into the forehead of your Goliath—if you trust them. The power of these truths is guaranteed, and they need only your faith in action to be realized. Just as in David's epic confrontation that changed history, so too your own spiritual fortunes and destiny are about to change. Your words and actions will betray all logic and common sense to those around you *exactly* because they are coming from a new well of personal conviction, relationship and loyalty previously unseen by others. The stake is going in the ground.

In this moment, clutching this stone, you are choosing to stand.

Kenny Luck
Author of *Sleeping Giant*
Men's Pastor at Saddleback Church
Founder of Every Man Ministries

PREFACE

Warning! The book you are about to read is rated PG-13, "For Men Only!" This is not a high and lofty spiritual treatise, nor is it a dry theological essay. I have written this book just like I would speak it to the men of my church.

It is not written to super-religious churchmen who have it all together. It is written to seekers who are eager to know God. It is written to pagans who have honest questions about faith. It is written to young Christians who are in the trenches of fighting the spiritual battle. It is written to spiritual veterans who are tired of having their butts kicked by the enemy.

If you are a narrow-minded fundamentalist, then you will be offended. If you are a legalistic Pharisee, then you will be offended. If you would rather argue about theology than really know God, then you will be offended. If you are hiding behind your unanswered religious questions, then you will be offended. If you are a wimp, then you will be offended. If you have to ask your wife's permission to read this book, then you will definitely be offended!

Here's a reality check: there are real Goliaths standing in your path. But the good news is that through Jesus Christ, the battle is the Lord's! Interested in finding out more? Read on!

INTRODUCTION

EVERY MAN IS ON A SPIRITUAL JOURNEY

I was sitting in the athletic team room at UCLA, surrounded by a group of football players from the Rose Bowl champion Bruins. (For you Trojan fans, yes, this was a long time ago!) We had gathered that evening for a meeting sponsored by Athletes in Action, an on-campus Christian group. As a young campus minister, it was my privilege to mentor many of the athletes on campus.

Our speaker that evening, a UCLA alumnus and NFL veteran, gazed over the heads of the young athletes and then pointed to a banner on the wall. The banner contained one word, spelled out in bold print: "PURSUIT." The speaker, with the voice of experience, began his message: "Pursuit—do you know what that means? It means to pursue it!" He went on to explain that the most important pursuit in life was not athletics but the pursuit of a relationship with God through Jesus Christ.

Years later, and much further down the path of my own journey, I absolutely agree with the words of that speaker. *Pursuing God through a relationship with Jesus Christ is the most important commitment a man can make.*

Every man is on a spiritual journey. You may be full of questions about God, the Bible and the Christian life, or you may be completely convinced of Christ's reality—either way, you are on a spiritual journey. Some men have traveled long on the path, while others aren't even aware that they are going anywhere; but God created each of us to know Him, and life is all about the pursuit. Reading this book may be the beginning of your journey to know God, or it may encourage you to keep moving forward. Wherever you are on your path, understanding the journey can empower you to take proactive steps in pursuing a relationship with Christ. The apostle Paul proclaimed:

> But whatever was to my profit I now consider loss for the sake of Christ. What is more, I consider everything a loss compared to the surpassing greatness of knowing Christ Jesus my Lord, for whose sake I have lost all things. I consider them rubbish, that I may gain Christ (Phil. 3:7-8).

Our pursuit must lead us to the knowledge of Jesus Christ, because knowing Jesus Christ is our ultimate purpose in life. I'm not talking about just head knowledge about God; I mean real, personal knowledge of God. The word Paul uses here in Philippians 3 is *epignosis*. This word describes an authentic, relational and experiential knowledge of something. In this case, it refers to the authentic, relational and experiential knowledge of Christ.

When my wife was pregnant with our first child, we decided to do natural childbirth. We took all the classes, and I assumed the role I was made for—the coach! I learned all about pregnancy, birth and proper breathing techniques.

I was the star student in our Lamaze class—although I was also a bit of a cut-up. I remember our teacher asking the class, "What is the pelvic rock?"

With a straight face, I replied, "Well, that's what got us here in the first place!" Needless to say, my wife didn't appreciate my humor.

Despite my jokes, I took the whole process very seriously. I read the manual, looked at the pictures, and was fully prepared for my wife's labor and delivery. We had decided to forego knowing the sex of our child and waited until delivery to find out if we were having a boy or a girl. Calm, cool and collected, I guided my wife through all the breathing techniques of natural childbirth. With learned precision, I did everything that was expected of me as a coach.

In the middle of the night, my wife awoke and shouted, "My water just broke!" Remembering our training, we calmly got ready, checked into the hospital, and awaited the birth of our first child. As the moment of delivery came, the doctor told my wife to give one last push. With herculean effort, my wife delivered our child.

The moment my son was born, I was overcome with the joy and wonder of birth. I had a son! All the reading, preparation and book knowledge paled in comparison with the actual experience of his birth. I didn't just know about the birth of my son; I personally experienced it.

There is a big difference between knowing about God and actually knowing God. Every man was created to personally know God—not just to know about Him but to actually know Him. Our greatest pursuit is the pursuit of God. When we know God through Jesus Christ, we come to share in His life. Jesus said, "The thief comes only to steal and kill and destroy; I came that they may have life, and have it abundantly" (John 10:10, *NASB*).

Would you like to experience abundant life? It is possible, if you pursue a relationship with Jesus Christ. This pursuit, however, has its challenges. In every man's spiritual journey, there is a thief who steals, kills and destroys. There are obstacles that must be overcome and giants that must be defeated. Pursuing Christ is going to involve a struggle. But what man doesn't like a good fight? As the apostle Paul admonishes us, "Fight the good fight of the faith. Take hold of the eternal life to which you were called" (1 Tim. 6:12).

As we begin to unpack the Bible's teaching concerning the pursuit of Christ, I am reminded of the words of my old football coach: "Men, put your chin straps on tight and let the snot fly!" With chinstraps in place and a generous spew of mucus in the air, let's examine the spiritual realities we can expect as we follow after Christ.

Discussion

See It

Read Philippians 3:7-14.

- Why do you think Paul was so obsessed with knowing Christ?
- What do you think drives most men?

Discuss It

- What do you think is the difference between knowing about Christ and truly knowing Christ?
- According to Philippians 3:7-8, what value did Paul place on knowing Christ?
- What would you put on a list of "things that are to your profit"? Do you think knowing Christ is of even more value than the things people most treasure?

Do It

- In your spiritual journey, what value do you place on knowing Christ?
- What would it look like for you to consider knowing Christ to be of more value than anything else in your life?
- Read Philippians 3:12-14. How did Paul prioritize knowing Christ? Based on Paul's example, what priority should knowing Christ have in your life?
- What is the next step in your journey?

1

THERE ARE GIANTS IN THE PATH

A few years ago, some friends and I attended the midnight opening of the movie *300*. I noticed only one female in a full theatre. Chick flick it wasn't! Why were men packing a theatre at midnight? Because most men like a good fight!

Men connect with the sights and sounds of battle; we feel it in our guts. We understand the thrill of victory and the agony of defeat.

When my son was 17, I asked him, "What's your favorite movie fight scene?" I offered him three options. The first was the opening scene from *The Rundown*, starring the Rock. In this scene, the Rock takes out the entire offensive line of a Super Bowl champion football team.

The second was the battle to the death between Maximus and Comidus in *Gladiator*. In this climactic fight, Maximus, played by Russell Crowe, endures a mortal wound, and yet still manages to defeat Comidus. It's a classic good guy versus bad guy battle.

The third choice I gave him was the scene in *The Patriot* where Benjamin Martin, played by Mel Gibson, takes out 20 British soldiers with a rifle and a tomahawk! Considering his options, my son reached a quick decision.

He chose the Rock in *The Rundown*. My son is a man. He likes fights!

One of the reasons I love the Old Testament is because it's a man's book. If Hollywood were to make the Old Testament into a feature film, it would definitely not be a romantic comedy. From Genesis to Malachi, it is filled with great fights. The Old

Testament records the good, the bad and the ugly of real men—
men who lived, fought and died as men.

My favorite fight in the Old Testament is found in 1 Samuel
17: the story of David and Goliath. Within the account, we find
this statement: "As the Philistine moved closer to attack him,
David ran quickly toward the battle line to meet him" (v. 48). Full
of testosterone and adrenaline, David ran balls-out and killed Goliath. David was a man who went after it. He knew God, and he
knew what God wanted him to do. You can't help but admire his
confidence and faith. But the battle didn't start with David.

The battle began in the Valley of Elah. King Saul and the entire Israelite army gathered together on one side of this historic
battleground. Arrayed in position opposite them were their gener-
ational enemies, the Philistines. Longtime rivals, the Israelites and
the Philistines fought more battles than Muhammad Ali and Joe
Frazier. As the commander of Israel's army, Saul had a track record
of being a fierce warrior. On this day, however, the Philistines used
a different tactic. Descending into the valley walked the largest
man any of the Israelites had ever seen. His name was Goliath.
Check out this description:

> So the Philistines and Israelites faced each other on oppo-
> site hills, with the valley between them. Then Goliath, a
> Philistine champion from Gath, came out of the Philis-
> tine ranks to face the forces of Israel. He was over nine
> feet tall! He wore a bronze helmet, and his bronze coat of
> mail weighed 125 pounds. He also wore bronze leg armor,
> and he carried a bronze javelin on his shoulder. The shaft
> of his spear was as heavy and thick as a weaver's beam,
> tipped with an iron spearhead that weighed 15 pounds.
> His armor bearer walked ahead of him carrying a shield
> (1 Sam. 17:3-7, NLT).

At over 9 feet tall, Goliath would make Shaq look like a pygmy!
His armor weighed 125 pounds, and the head of his spear weighed
15 pounds. As I write this, I weigh about 200 pounds (in case my

wife is reading this, I should admit that I am exaggerating for literary purposes and am really a svelte 185 pounds!). That means that Goliath's armor alone was more than half my body weight. He was, without a doubt, the scariest dude who ever lived.

In the opening scene of the movie *Troy*, Brad Pitt, playing the role of Achilles, fights a giant of a man named Boagrius. Boagrius bursts through the ranks of the Aegean army and literally fills the movie screen with his sheer size. Standing at least a head taller than the other warriors, he very much looks the part of the biggest, baddest fighter around. Nathan Jones, the actor who portrays Boagrius, is 7 feet tall and weighs 350 pounds—convincingly a very big man. Goliath, however, was over 9 feet tall! If Achilles's challenger caused a hush in the Greek army, you can understand why complete terror rippled across the Israelite troops when Goliath stepped into the Elah Valley and issued this challenge:

> Goliath stood and shouted to the ranks of Israel, "Why do you come out and line up for battle? Am I not a Philistine, and are you not the servants of Saul? Choose a man and have him come down to me. If he is able to fight and kill me, we will become your subjects; but if I overcome him and kill him, you will become our subjects and serve us." Then the Philistine said, "This day I defy the ranks of Israel! Give me a man and let us fight each other." On hearing the Philistine's words, Saul and all the Israelites were dismayed and terrified (1 Sam. 17:8-11).

"Dismayed and terrified." There it is—fear. Fear is the most debilitating emotion to man's masculinity. It robs us of what we feel it means to be a man.

The men of Israel were intimidated. They were afraid. It was a primal emotion that gripped them from the core of their being. They encountered their giant and it scared them to death. Every man has a Goliath. Every man faces a giant at some point during his journey. Every man stares down into the Elah Valley—and what he sees staring back is terrifying. *Every man has to contend with giants if he is going to press on and experience a life-transforming relationship with Jesus Christ.*

Your giant could be intellectual doubt. You want to believe in God. You want to live by faith and have confidence that God is real and in charge of your life. You understand how much simpler it would be to trust the Bible and the promises of Jesus. If you could believe in heaven and a final judgment, then maybe all the evil around you could have some ultimate meaning. The message of the gospel seems compelling, but you just can't commit yourself to believe it. You have unanswered questions and nagging doubts about whether it's true. If this is you, your giant is intellectual doubt.

Your giant could be fear. You are deathly afraid of something—change, the unknown, being unloved, being found out, failure, or any number of other things. You easily identify with the Israelite army. Fear has dominated your life. You are passive-aggressive, trying to stay under the radar because of your crippling fear. If this is you, your giant is fear.

Your giant could be pride. You love the fact that you are in control of your own life and answer to no one. You know you're not perfect, but inside you are confident that you're better than most. Frank Sinatra's "I Did It My Way" is your personal theme song. You know you should be more humble, but you tend to believe your own press releases. You may have the worst kind of pride—religious pride; you think you are more spiritual than others. Though you wouldn't admit it, you privately think, *God's pretty lucky to have me on His side.* If this is you, your giant is pride.

Your giant could be lust. You find yourself fantasizing about every pretty girl you meet, and even some of the not-so-pretty ones! You want to be pure-minded—and if you're married, you want to be faithful to your wife—but at the same time, you feel enslaved to sexual thoughts. You may carry a secret shame over a part of your life that is both repulsive and exciting at the same time. And if it's not sexual lust, it's just personal selfishness. You look out for number one! Self is deeply enthroned in your life. If this is you, your giant is lust.

Your giant could be anger. You get up every morning registering a 9+ on the 10-point anger scale. Every frustration, blocked goal or personal inconvenience seems to send you over the edge. If you are not erupting like a volcano, then you are on a slow burn of passive-aggressive emotion. The people in your life behave like they are walking on broken glass as they desperately seek not to fuel your volatility. If this is you, your giant is anger.

Every man has a giant. Like Goliath did to Saul and the army of Israel, our giant taunts us and challenges us every day. But remember, the story of David and Goliath ends victoriously. This story gives us hope that we can win our spiritual battles and pursue the life God has planned for us as men. When David faced Goliath, fear was turned into faith through God's strength:

> Then he [David] took his staff in his hand, chose five smooth stones from the stream, put them in the pouch of his shepherd's bag and, with his sling in his hand, approached the Philistine.
>
> Meanwhile, the Philistine, with his shield bearer in front of him, kept coming closer to David. He looked David over and saw that he was only a boy, ruddy and handsome, and he despised him. He said to David, "Am I a dog, that you come at me with sticks?" And the Philistine cursed David by his gods. "Come here," he said, "and I'll give your flesh to the birds of the air and the beasts of the field!"
>
> David said to the Philistine, "You come against me with sword and spear and javelin, but I come against you in the name of the LORD Almighty, the God of the armies of Israel, whom you have defied. This day the LORD will hand you over to me, and I'll strike you down and cut off your head. Today I will give the carcasses of the Philistine army to the birds of the air and the beasts of the earth, and the whole world will know that there is a God in Israel. All those gathered here will know that it is not by sword or spear that the LORD saves; for the battle is the LORD's, and he will give all of you into our hands."
>
> As the Philistine moved closer to attack him, David ran quickly toward the battle line to meet him. Reaching

into his bag and taking out a stone, he slung it and struck the Philistine on the forehead. The stone sank into his forehead, and he fell facedown on the ground.

So David triumphed over the Philistine with a sling and a stone; without a sword in his hand he struck down the Philistine and killed him (1 Sam. 17:40–50).

Unlike Saul and all the soldiers of Israel, David looked at Goliath through a God-sized lens rather than looking at God through a Goliath-sized lens. David "declared that the battle belonged to the Lord"—and then he literally ran to meet the giant. Let's look at verse 48 one more time: "As the Philistine moved closer to attack him, David ran quickly toward the battle line to meet him." That's my favorite verse in this story. David ran toward Goliath. David pursued God's plan for his life. Don't you love that?

On my desk, I have a little rock taken from the Elah Valley in Israel. This rock is inscribed with a simple sentence: "And David ran." David kept his focus on God, and that produced a confident faith.

I want to be a man like David. I want to run to meet the giants in my life and defeat them in the Lord's strength. Every man can run to battle. Every man can pursue a relationship with Christ—but in order to do so, he must focus on God and His unlimited resources, and not be defeated by the giants in his path.

In the next few chapters, we will look at the five main giants every man faces: intellectual doubt, fear, pride, lust and anger. We will see how these giants are obstacles that stand in the way of following Christ and experiencing spiritual victory. We will also learn how to overcome these giants with the truth and power of the gospel. Armed with the truth, we will wrap up this book with a positive game plan for pursuing after Christ. But before we look at the specific giants we face, we are going to take a closer look at the Goliath behind all of our giants.

Some of this discussion may feel overwhelming, but hang in there. Wherever you are in your spiritual journey, there is a victorious path to follow.

Discussion

See It

Read 1 Samuel 17:1-11,16,23-24.

- How does this passage describe Goliath and the impact he had on the men of Israel?

- What is the gut response most men have when they face a giant in their spiritual path?

Discuss It

- Giants have the potential to stop us in our spiritual progress. Read the following passages and discuss the reality of spiritual opposition and its ultimate source: Matthew 4:1-11; Ephesians 6:10-13; 1 Peter 5:8-9; 2 Corinthians 4:3-4.

- Since spiritual opposition is a reality, look up the following passages and discuss some of the giants that every man can anticipate facing: Mark 4:13-19; 1 John 2:15-17; 1 Timothy 6:9-12; 2 Samuel 11:1-5; Joshua 1:6-9.

Do It

- What kind of preparations can a man make in his life so that he will be ready to face and defeat his giants?

- How do these verses give us the hope of victory over our giants: 1 Corinthians 15:57; Romans 9:31-39; 2 Corinthians 2:14?

- What will you do as a result of this study to live today and every day in Christ's victory?

2

WHAT'S YOUR GOLIATH?

Pursuing after Jesus Christ is more than an intellectual inquiry into Christianity. It is a spiritual journey, with spiritual questions and answers. Some of you old guys might remember the movie *Monty Python and the Holy Grail*. There is a scene in the movie where King Arthur and his entourage are interrogated by a troll-like creature before they can cross a mountain bridge. The bridge-keeper asks each person who wants to cross the bridge odd questions— and their answers determine whether they will pass or be hurled to their death. When Lancelot, one of Arthur's knights, approaches the bridge-keeper, the question is: "What is your quest?"

Lancelot answers, "To seek the Holy Grail."

The pursuit of a relationship with Jesus Christ, like the pursuit of the Holy Grail, is a quest—complete with mountain bridges and formidable obstacles. The Bible is clear that there is an enemy who seeks to distort the truth, deceiving and enslaving every man. Each of us must face the giants that oppose us.

According to 1 Samuel 17:1-24, Goliath taunted the armies of Israel day after day, for 40 days. His relentless intimidation robbed the Israelites of any courageous fighting spirit. Outraged by Goliath's pagan accusation of Israel and its God, David accepted the giant's challenge and descended into the Valley of Elah. Every man has an Elah Valley. Like Goliath of old, our giants confront us daily. Each of us must contend with the lust of the flesh, the lust of the eyes, and the boastful pride of life. We all know the reality of failure and personal struggle. We have faced giants in the past and we will face them in the future.

In his novel *The Killer Angels*, Michael Shaara describes the small events that made up the larger confrontation of the Battle of

Gettysburg. Shaara re-creates the rifle exchanges and bayonet charges in the struggle for control of a tiny piece of turf known as Little Round Top. This seemingly insignificant fight is used to illustrate how the whole of the battle can be brought down to the experience of each and every individual soldier. Like an infantryman in the battle for Little Round Top, the Bible says that every man is a warrior in a cosmic spiritual struggle. The skirmishes we face on a daily basis are merely small parts of a larger war that is taking place.

If you have never studied the Bible, the concept of Satan and spiritual warfare might seem far-fetched. It may strike you like a fantasy similar to *Lord of the Rings*. Believe me, I understand your skepticism. But before you check out intellectually, please give me a minute to unpack what the Bible teaches about spiritual warfare. Hopefully I can connect the dots so that you can see how this invisible battle relates to a man overcoming his giants and pursuing a relationship with God.

As we read in Mark 4:1-20, Jesus compared experiencing God and His kingdom to a farmer planting seeds. The point of this parable was to show that just as a seed's fruitfulness is determined by the quality of the soil it lands in, so too will a person's response to God's message be determined by the kind of heart he has. When Jesus was explaining the parable to His disciples, He made it clear that He is the farmer who plants the seed of God's message. Our hearts, the deepest part of our personality, represent the soil that receives the seed. Depending upon the kind of heart we have, the seed either bears fruit or it doesn't.

Jesus teaches that there are four kinds of spiritual soil (in other words, hearts): hard, rocky, weed-infested and good. It is the good heart that receives, believes and applies God's message. Describing the hard soil, Jesus says:

> The farmer sows the word. Some people are like seed along the path, where the word is sown. As soon as they hear it, Satan comes and takes away the word that was sown in them (Mark 4:14-15).

Jesus tells us that Satan snatches or takes away the word before it can be received and transform a person's life. Believing in God and following Christ is a spiritual experience that involves overcoming spiritual obstacles. To successfully overcome those obstacles, we need to hear from God—but Satan takes away the word by deceiving men and influencing them to reject the truth of the gospel.

Several months ago, I had gone to the gym to work out and was following my exercise with a relaxing time in the Jacuzzi. I had an old Bible with me, and I was reading through the Gospel of Mark. Out of the corner of my eye, I could see that another guy sitting in the Jacuzzi was watching me read the Bible. After a few minutes, he spoke up and asked, "What are you reading?"

Without much engagement, I responded, "The Bible."

After a few more minutes, he asked, "Where in the Bible are you reading?"

Again pleasantly but with minimal words, I responded, "The Gospel of Mark."

This was followed by a short pause, and then he asked, "What are you learning?"

I put the Bible down on the concrete, smiled and said, "OK, but remember you asked me." I told him about the parable of the four soils and Jesus' description of the human heart. Then I asked him, "What kind of soil are you? Where is your heart with God?"

Jesus' teaching is very simple and very practical: Some people have hard hearts, and the reason is that the devil has influenced their unbelief with a spiritual blindness.

Along the same lines, the apostle Paul wrote to the Corinthian church:

> And even if our gospel is veiled, it is veiled to those who are perishing. The god of this age has blinded the minds of unbelievers, so that they cannot see the light of the gospel of the glory of Christ, who is the image of God (2 Cor. 4:3-4).

The god of this age—Satan—blinds the minds of the unbelieving so that they cannot see the light of the gospel in Christ. *Satan*

*is real—and his mission is to stop you from surrendering your life to God
and receiving Jesus Christ as your Savior. If he is unsuccessful in his plan
A—preventing you from giving your life to Christ and receiving salvation—
then he resorts to plan B—attacking you in your Christian journey and seeking to keep you from truly knowing God.*

A couple of years ago, I had the privilege of traveling to South
Africa on a men's mission trip. After 10 days in the Cape Town
area, we ended our journey with a photo-safari in Kruger Park—
one of the largest game reserves in Africa. On our first morning in
the park, several of us got up at 0-dark hundred to board specially
designed Jeeps and venture into the bush. The sun was just rising
above the horizon when we came upon herds of gazelle, wilde-
beests and zebra that roamed with barely an acknowledgment of
our presence. Suddenly, without warning, I could sense something
change in the attitude of the animals.

I felt it before I heard it—a roar reverberating in the cool damp
air. Boldly ambling down the middle of the road, a male lion approached the grazing animals. There it was again: A loud roar
cracked the atmosphere and all the animals scattered in every direction. The lion's hot breath in the moist air created a mist
shrouding his gaping mouth. Slowly our Jeep moved parallel
with the fluidly approaching lion. Matching its speed, we drove
practically unnoticed next to the animal's taut, muscular body.
As I sat on the outer edge of the Jeep, I was very much aware that
with his lightning quick reflexes, the lion could have attacked
me without notice.

The lion's dominance on the scene, with both the other animals and the passengers in the Jeep, left no doubt that he was the
King of Beasts! The mere roar of the lion caused pandemonium in
the otherwise pastoral setting. The effect a lion has on his potential prey serves as a backdrop to Peter's words in 1 Peter 5:8: "Be on
the alert. Your adversary, the devil, prowls around like a roaring
lion, seeking someone to devour" (*NASB*). We have an enemy more
intimidating than any physical lion, and he wants to devour us.

Jesus said, "The thief comes only to steal and kill and destroy;
I came that they may have life, and have it abundantly" (John

10:10, *NASB*). The abundant life that Jesus offers every man is presented in contrast to the stealing, killing and destroying of the thief. Satan wants to rob men of discovering a personal relationship with Jesus Christ. He wants to kill a man's conviction for following Christ, and he wants to destroy a man's faith. Satan is the ultimate Goliath. Directly and indirectly, every man goes toe to toe with the adversary in the Valley of Elah.

In his letter to the Ephesians, the apostle Paul warns of the reality of the spiritual battle:

> Finally, be strong in the Lord and in his mighty power. Put on the full armor of God so that you can take your stand against the devil's schemes. For our struggle is not against flesh and blood, but against the rulers, against the authorities, against the powers of this dark world and against the spiritual forces of evil in the heavenly realms. Therefore put on the full armor of God, so that when the day of evil comes, you may be able to stand your ground, and after you have done everything, to stand (Eph. 6:10-13).

Paul writes, "*Finally*, be strong in the Lord" (emphasis added). In other words, everything he has written up to this point has its application in this final charge—which is a call to fight and win the spiritual battle. Every man is engaged in conflict. According to the Bible, our battle is not against flesh and blood, but against Satan and his demons. Paul refers to this satanic strike force as "rulers," "authorities," "powers of this dark world," and "spiritual forces of evil in the heavenly realms." This passage describes a demonic hierarchy that is unleashed to attack and destroy believers. But remember, Satan is not equal to God. He is not omnipresent nor is he omniscient. He is a powerful but limited angel. He is a created being who has at his disposal a host of demonic angels to do his bidding.

Every man's ultimate Goliath is our adversary, the devil. Our Elah Valley—the battleground—is the culture in which we live, and the point of attack is our heart. The term "heart," as used in the Bible, represents the deepest part of our personhood. It is where we make our moral decisions, embrace our core beliefs, and choose our deepest loves. The Bible exhorts us, "Above all else, guard your heart, for it is the wellspring of life" (Prov. 4:23). Everything about who we are, what we love, and what we are committed to flows out of our heart. It is in the thoughts of our heart that we wrestle with our biggest giants. Our doubts, fears, lusts, accusations and objections take place in the heart. Out of our heart, we choose either to reject Christ and His plan of salvation or to surrender to God and dynamically follow Christ. The prophet Jeremiah asserts:

> The heart is deceitful above all things and beyond cure. Who can understand it? "I the LORD search the heart and examine the mind, to reward a man according to his conduct, according to what his deeds deserve" (Jer. 17:9-10).

We don't have clarity about our hearts—only God truly knows us at that level. That is why our hearts are vulnerable to spiritual struggles, relational conflicts and self-doubt. We conquer our giants when our hearts are surrendered to God and we are pursuing after Christ.

Our battle with our giants wages most intensely in our thought life. We can think great thoughts about God and gain confidence in our faith—or we can give in to doubt and temptation and become like the Israelites, who were paralyzed by fear. Commenting on the power of our thoughts, Paul says:

> Those who live according to the sinful nature have their *minds* set on what that nature desires; but those who live in accordance with the Spirit have their *minds* set on what the Spirit desires. The *mind* of sinful man is death, but the *mind* controlled by the Spirit is life and peace; the sinful *mind* is hostile to God. It does not submit to God's law, nor can it do so (Rom. 8:5-7, emphasis added).

Notice Paul's emphasis on the mind. What we allow to control our minds and fill our thoughts shapes our perspective on life. Inevitably, our thoughts influence our words and actions. When the giants of doubt, fear, pride, lust or anger capture our minds, they gain momentum in our life like a ball rolling down hill. Our thoughts are the key to both our conflicts and our victories.

Picture it this way: You are on a camping trip with a couple of buddies. There is no purified water, so you need to boil water to drink. You set up your Coleman stove, light the gas, and put on a pot of water. Pretty soon the water boils, and steam starts to leak out from the pot. Let's say, for the sake of argument, that you don't want any steam to escape from the pot. So, you find a lid and put it on top of the boiling water. This works for a while, but as the pressure builds in the pot, steam inevitably escapes. You can try to find a heavier lid, but what else could you do to stop steam from coming out of the pot? That's right, turn off the heat! Here's the analogy: The fire represents our thoughts, the water represents our emotions, and the steam represents our actions. The fire of our thoughts boils the water of our emotions, which then produces the steam of our actions. What we think about controls our feelings and influences our behavior. There is an inseparable relationship between our thoughts, our feelings and our actions.

Remember the story of David and Goliath? Saul and the Israelite army saw Goliath as huge and terrifying; therefore God looked small. Their thoughts generated feelings of fear and led them to passivity and inaction. David, on the other hand, had huge thoughts of God, which made Goliath look small. His thoughts inspired confidence and led to faith-driven action. Our thoughts represent the means by which our giants attack us—and also the means by which we must fight back. When doubt, fear, pride, lust and anger rear their ugly heads, they do so with a whole array of thoughts that are designed to defeat us. Recognizing that the battle is being fought in the thoughts of our hearts is the first step in facing and conquering our giants.

According to the Gospel of John, "Jesus said to those Jews who believed Him, 'If you abide in My word, you are My disciples indeed. And you shall know the truth, and the truth shall make you free'" (John 8:31-32, *NKJV*).

Abiding in Jesus' Word is a qualification for being one of His disciples. True followers of Jesus accept His Word, believe His Word, and practice His Word. Jesus' Word is the truth that sets us free. Every man either believes the truth and is set free, or believes a lie and is held in bondage.

Giants lie to us. The Goliath of doubt lies to us, and we believe that there is no evidence for trusting in Jesus Christ. The Goliath of fear lies to us, and we are intimidated by our circumstances. The Goliath of pride lies to us, and we believe our own press releases. The Goliath of lust lies to us, and we believe we must have the object of our desire. The Goliath of anger lies to us, and we feel fully justified in venting our feelings. Every man faces Goliath, because every man deals with the giants of his own thought life. It is only as we accept the truth of Jesus Christ and abide in His Word that we can conquer our giants.

David was a man just like us, and he conquered his giant. Not only was David a warrior, but he was also a poet and a songwriter. Many of his poems and songs are recorded in the Bible in the book of Psalms. These psalms are the personalized reflections of David as he meditated on God and His Word. David thought great thoughts about God. He prayed great prayers to God. And he attempted great things for God. David ran into battle because he knew the battle belonged to the Lord. Like David, we need to renew our minds with the truth. When we think on and believe in the power and grace of Jesus Christ, our giants begin to look small. It is the truth of Christ and His Word that sets us free. Every man faces giants—and every man can conquer them if he knows the truth.

Several years ago, my daughter watched a scary movie with some really intense scenes. As she was preparing for bed, she told me she was afraid she would have bad dreams. Part of our ritual at bedtime was to read the Bible and pray together. On this occasion, I suggested that she read 1 Samuel 17. I waited about 15 minutes and then went into her room to pray. Our conversation went something like this:

J. P.: "So what did you think of 1 Samuel 17?"
Ashton: "It's the story of David and Goliath, Daddy."

J. P.: "What did the Israelites do when they saw Goliath?"

Ashton: "They were afraid to fight."

J. P.: "Do you know why?"

Ashton: "Goliath looked too big."

J. P.: "Do you think he was too big for God?"

Ashton: "No."

J. P.: "Were the Israelites looking at God, or were they looking at Goliath?"

Ashton: "They were looking at Goliath."

J. P.: "What about David? Who did he look at?"

Ashton: "He looked at God."

J. P.: "How do you know?"

Ashton: "Because David said that the battle belonged to God, and that God was going to help him win."

J. P.: "That's right, and because David had his faith in God, Goliath looked small."

I went on to explain that if she woke up in the middle of the night from a bad dream, she should think about how big God is. She should remind herself that He is powerful and that He loves her. She should remember that God is her protector and that Jesus lives inside of her and will never leave her. We prayed, and she slept soundly that night.

My daughter was 12 years old, and she understood the reality of the spiritual battle. She also understood the power of the truth to conquer her giants.

Satan wants to defeat us in our thought life. He wants to enslave us through the Goliaths of doubt, fear, pride, lust and anger. God, on the other hand, wants to set us free. He wants to renew our minds and give us spiritual victory. Remember Romans 8:6: "For the mind set on the flesh is death, but the mind set on the Spirit is life and peace" (*NASB*). We get to choose what we think about and what we believe. We can abide in the Word of Jesus Christ and be set free, or we can be victims of our own giants.

Pursuing after Jesus Christ takes dogged determination. Every man must choose to press on and overcome any obstacle that stands in his way. When I was in high school, the state champion sprinter in the 100- and 220-yard dashes competed in our league. His name was Millard Hampton, and he went on to receive a gold medal in the Olympics. Coming in second to Hampton in the league competition was a track athlete from my high school named Winston Wingfield. Winston wasn't as fast as Millard Hampton, but he was pretty quick—and he gave his all when he ran.

When our senior yearbook came out, all the members of the Lettermen Club looked to the sports section to see if they could find any pictures of themselves. In the Track section, there were photos of Winston winning various competitions. One picture, however, seemed a little odd. If you looked at it long enough, the oddity became apparent. The picture was of Winston in full stride—and noticeably on his thigh, protruding from his skimpy track shorts, was male genitalia. That's right; Winston was literally running balls-out! Metaphorically, that's the only way to win a competition—and the only way to pursue a relationship with Christ. We are to seek after Christ, in spite of the obstacles, with every bit of intellectual, emotional and willful energy we have.

One of the great privileges of being a man is our God-given masculine energy. Most men waste or abuse their masculinity. God wants us to use the energy He has given us to invest in a life-long pursuit of Jesus Christ and His kingdom. The promise of God is clear:

> "For I know the plans I have for you," declares the LORD, "plans to prosper you and not to harm you, plans to give you hope and a future. Then you will call upon me and come and pray to me, and I will listen to you. You will seek me and find me when you seek me with all your heart" (Jer. 29:11-13).

When we seek God, we find Him. If we will run balls-out in our pursuit of Jesus Christ, then we will gain the knowledge of God and be transformed to become men like Jesus.

As in any journey, the key is to keep putting one foot in front of the other. One thing that can slow us down and even stop our forward progress completely is intellectual doubt. To keep going after Jesus, we must be convinced that the gospel is true and that His Word is reliable. In the next chapter, we will discover how to defeat the Goliath of Intellectual Doubt.

Discussion

See It

Read 1 Samuel 17:1-11,41-51.

- How would you describe the giant that David faced?

- Every man must face his own Goliath(s). What are some of the Goliaths that men face?

Discuss It

- Read the following verses and discuss some of the Goliaths that men face: Ephesians 6:10-13; 2 Samuel 11:1-5; 1 John 2:15-17; James 4:1-7.

- The Bible reveals that the archetype of all Goliaths is Satan. How do you feel about this statement? What do you think about the reality of spiritual warfare?

- In this chapter, I suggest five main Goliaths that men face: doubt, fear, pride, lust and anger. Discuss each of these and comment on how they can be Goliaths in men's lives.

Do It

- When we face a Goliath, do you think we are helpless victims? How can a man surrender to God and experience God's help for victory?

- What is your next step in facing and defeating the Goliaths in your life?

3

FACING THE GOLIATH OF INTELLECTUAL DOUBT

My son was a two-sport athlete in high school, competing in both football and wrestling. Unlike football, wrestling is an individual sport. When your match is called, it's just you and your opponent on the mat. One of the schools in my son's league was a private Christian school, Calvary Chapel. For years, Calvary Chapel has been one of the best wrestling schools in the state of California. These young men are not only outstanding athletes but also dedicated Christians. During my son's junior season, one of the Calvary Chapel wrestlers was a returning California state champ and eventual national champion.

On the night of their meet, I sat in the stands with some other dads. Seeing a familiar face, I asked, "Who is your son wrestling tonight?" In the corner of the gym was the soon-to-be national champion. He was a man-child with a massive neck and bulging biceps. He wore a shirt with bold black letters: JESUS.

In response to my question, the other dad stammered, pointed to the corner of the gym, and blurted out, "Jesus!"

I laughed and said, "If your son is wrestling Jesus, then he is going to lose for sure." That night, everyone's focus was on Jesus—as ours should be every day if we want to defeat our Goliaths.

We grow strong in our faith when we put our focus on Jesus Christ. The apostle Peter understood this when he walked on water (see Matt. 14:22-33). Do you remember this miracle? In the middle of the night, Jesus stepped off terra firma, strolled across the Sea of Galilee, and met the disciples adrift in their boat. There were actually two miracles: the first was Jesus walking on water, and the second was

Peter walking on water! Focusing his attention on Jesus and obeying Jesus' command, Peter stepped out of the boat and began to walk on the surface of the water. As the text tells us, however, Peter soon began to feel the wind and look at the waves, taking his eyes off of Jesus. When he did this, he began to sink! Like Peter, when we look to Jesus, we grow strong in faith. Also like Peter, when we take our eyes off of Jesus, faith is overcome by unbelief. Where is your focus today? Are you looking at your giant or are you looking at God? Defeating the giants and pursuing Christ takes a God-sized focus.

What we believe about God determines whether we live by fear or by faith. What is your view of God? Biblical faith begins with a proper view of God: "Without faith it is impossible to please God, because anyone who comes to him must believe that he exists and that he rewards those who earnestly seek Him" (Heb. 11:6). Living by faith means that we believe God is who He says He is. You cannot trust someone if you don't know them. A man would never hand the keys of his brand-new car over to a stranger on the street and say, "Drive it all you want and bring it back to me at the end of the day." No, a reasonable man would want some assurances that his car was going to be handled properly. Trust, another word for faith, is always in proportion to our knowledge. To have faith in God, we must know who He is and what He has promised.

Faith holds on to what is true about God and then acts on His promises. Faith is always active. David had a track record with God. He had seen how God was faithful in the past, and he believed that God was also going to be faithful in the present. David put his faith into practice and faced his giant. He knew that the battle belonged to the Lord, so he ran to battle!

On the day that David ran to battle, thousands of Israelites stood paralyzed with fear. David saw Goliath and grew strong in faith, but those around him were frozen in their tracks because of doubt. Intellectual doubt can be a giant that neutralizes a man's pursuit of God. I have discovered that the heart cannot rejoice in what the mind rejects. Faith must have facts to back it up.

Many people liken faith to "taking a blind leap." Their understanding is that faith means you believe something even though there is no evidence to back up the belief. In fact, there's an odd idea out there that in order for faith to be faith, there must be a complete absence of fact to back it up. This notion is completely foreign to the Bible. The kind of faith described in the Bible is not faith in spite of the evidence but faith *in the evidence!*

Some time ago, I was at the gym working out and, as is my custom, I finished my workout by spending some time in the Jacuzzi. Next to the Jacuzzi was a lap pool where a young man was swimming with obvious skill and experience. When he had finished, I asked him if he was a competitive swimmer. "No, I play water polo at the community college." We talked for a while about water polo, and then I asked him what he was studying in school. "I'm a philosophy major and right now I am writing a paper on Soren Kierkegaard." Knowing a little bit about Kierkegaard, I asked the young man if he knew that Kierkegaard was a Christian. "Well, I knew he was religious, but I don't know that much about his faith."

I explained to him that Kierkegaard is known for being an existentialist and is credited with coining the phrase "Religion is a blind leap of faith." I went on to explain that the way Kierkegaard used that phrase is much different from the way people use it today. Kierkegaard was trying to move people to have a heart-felt faith and not merely an intellectually dead orthodoxy. Today we use the phrase to imply that religion has no basis in intellectual fact.

This young man was either humoring me or genuinely interested, because he asked me, "Well, aren't faith and facts mutually exclusive?" My response surprised him. I explained that biblical faith was based upon evidence. We are to put our faith in the facts—not exercise faith in spite of the facts.

I went on to explain that the gospel of Jesus Christ was a message asserting key historical, theological and spiritual propositions. These propositions were either true or they were false. Biblical faith was accepting the truth of the gospel, personalizing that truth, and acting in accord with it. We were outside, by the pool, so I pointed to a nearby bench and asked, "What if I told you all the specifications that went into making that bench? What if I had proof that the bench was made of reliable material and had been tested in the factory to hold the weight of a 500-pound person?"

The young man listened and said, "Okay."

I then asked him, "Do you think that bench could support your weight if you sat on it?"

He reasoned out loud, "Well, I weigh about 200 pounds, so sure, it would support me."

"Do you have faith that if you sat on the bench it would support you?"

"Yeah, I believe it," he answered.

I just stared at him for a while. It began to feel a little awkward. I looked at him and then at the bench and said, "I don't think you have faith that the bench will support your weight."

"No," he replied, "I believe it."

Still staring at him, I said, "You don't have biblical faith."

He thought for a moment and then walked over to the bench and sat down.

"Aha!" I blurted out, "*Now* you have biblical faith!"

I explained that biblical faith was action based upon evidence. It was being persuaded by the truth intellectually, receiving that truth emotionally, and acting on that truth volitionally. If we do not know the facts of the gospel, or if we doubt the veracity of the facts, our faith will be either non-existent or weak and anemic.

The way to strengthen faith is to study up on the facts. Our enemy knows this. Goliath is a deceiver, and one of his methods of attack is to create doubt. He treats us like we are mushrooms—he leaves us in the dark, feeding on manure! When we encounter intellectual doubt, we need to go back to the truth of the gospel: Jesus Christ lived, died and rose again. Christianity is true because Jesus is true. Doubt grows in an environment of ignorance. Faith flourishes in an environment of truth. Jesus said, "You will know the truth, and the truth will set you free" (John 8:32). The apostle Paul wrote, "Faith comes by hearing, and hearing by the word of Christ" (Rom. 10:17). When we saturate our minds with God's Word, the truth sets us free, and doubt is replaced by faith.

Paul illustrates this paradigm of putting our faith in the facts in his first letter to the Corinthians. He devotes the entire fifteenth chapter of this epistle to the truth of Christ's resurrection. In effect, Paul says that the resurrection is the quintessential truth that proves the reliability of Christianity and dispels all doubts:

> For what I received I passed on to you as of first importance: that Christ died for our sins according to the Scriptures, that he was buried, that he was raised on the third day according to the Scriptures, and that he appeared to Peter, and then to the Twelve. After that, he appeared to more than five hundred of the brothers at the same time, most of whom are still living, though some have fallen asleep. Then he appeared to James, then to all the apostles, and last of all he appeared to me also, as to one abnormally born. For I am the least of the apostles and do not even deserve to be called an apostle, because I persecuted the church of God. But by the grace of God I am what I am, and his grace to me was not without effect. No, I worked harder than all of them—yet not I, but the grace of God that was with me. Whether, then, it was I or they, this is what we preach, and this is what you believed (1 Cor. 15:3-11).

The most important truths of the gospel are that Christ died for our sins and that He was raised from the dead. Paul describes the various eyewitnesses to Christ's resurrection. This was not a mythological story but a historical fact. Paul himself had an encounter with the resurrected Christ. The gospel he preached—the gospel these early Christians believed—was a gospel based upon the facts of Christ's death and resurrection.

Paul goes on to explain why the fact of Christ's resurrection is essential to the gospel. His argument is that it is not enough that we believe it happened; the resurrection must be true for our faith to be potent and transformative. Faith must have a reliable object. We put our faith in the facts! In 1 Corinthians 15:12-19, Paul develops his thesis:

But if it is preached that Christ has been raised from the dead, how can some of you say that there is no resurrection of the dead? If there is no resurrection of the dead, then not even Christ has been raised. And if Christ has not been raised, our preaching is useless and so is your faith. More than that, we are then found to be false witnesses about God, for we have testified about God that he raised Christ from the dead. But he did not raise him if in fact the dead are not raised. For if the dead are not raised, then Christ has not been raised either. And if Christ has not been raised, your faith is futile; you are still in your sins. Then those also who have fallen asleep in Christ are lost. If only for this life we have hope in Christ, we are to be pitied more than all men.

Paul begins by assuming the perspective of the skeptic. If there is no such thing as "resurrection from the dead," then a specific example of a resurrection could never have happened. Paul argues from the larger premise to the smaller premise. If there is no category of miraculous resurrections, then any supposed phenomenon presenting itself as a resurrection could not exist.

This is precisely the philosophy of Naturalism. Materialistic Naturalism denies the supernatural, asserts that we live in a closed system, and explains all phenomena based upon data that exists within the system. Naturalism denies the existence of God, rejects the gospel, and asserts that there are no miracles. If a person subscribes to this worldview, he would consider the idea of the resurrection of Christ to be preposterous. This conclusion, however, would not be based on the evidence but on the philosophical worldview that interprets the evidence. Naturalist's reject and/or doubt the resurrection of Christ because they have a preconceived view that slants their understanding of the facts.

Paul continues his argument by discussing the implications of rejecting Christ's resurrection. If Christ was not raised from the dead, then preaching and faith are useless; they have no value or eternal impact. If Christ was not raised from the dead, then Paul and the other apostles were false witnesses. They said they saw Christ after His resurrection—so if He wasn't raised, then they are liars. If Christ was not raised from the dead, then our faith is futile and those of us who have trusted in Christ are still stuck in our sins. If Christ was not raised from the dead, then those who have fallen asleep—Paul's euphemism for death—are lost forever. Paul states that if we have hoped in Christ's resurrection, but it did not actually happen, then we should be pitied. His point is to demonstrate that it is not enough simply to believe that it happened. Our faith is not in our faith; our faith is in the facts of Christ's death and resurrection. The life-changing power behind our faith is that it is rooted in the truth. It is the truth that sets us free—and it is the truth that defeats the Goliath of intellectual doubt.

Understanding the nature and power of the truth, Paul responds to his straw man argument by affirming the fact of Christ's resurrection. This is the foundation of Christianity:

> But Christ has indeed been raised from the dead, the first-fruits of those who have fallen asleep. For since death came through a man, the resurrection of the dead comes also through a man. For as in Adam all die, so in Christ all will be made alive (1 Cor. 15:20-22).

Intellectual doubt must be brought to the court of truth. When we entertain our doubts, they become debilitating fears—and our Goliath bullies us into rejection of Christ. Honest doubts melt away when they are doused with the truth of God's Word and historical fact. Christ has been raised. His resurrection was attested to by numerous eyewitnesses. Paul himself encountered the resurrected Christ. Because Christ has been raised, and because we have put our faith in Christ, His truth sets us free.

Some may say, "But you are merely accepting the Bible's answer. You're not exploring all the other options." To be sure, many who reject Christ have tried to explain away the biblical account of Christ's resurrection. So, we must ask, "What do the facts support?" The evidence for Christ's death and resurrection can be found in each of the four Gospels of the New Testament. As well, the book of Acts and the New Testament letters attest to the fact that the disciples of Jesus believed in—and preached to others—Christ's resurrection. The objective seeker and the man struggling with doubt should look at the historical facts and reach an intelligent decision based upon the evidence.

According to the Bible, the critical facts concerning the death and resurrection of Jesus are the following:

- The Hebrew Scriptures (Old Testament) predict the death and resurrection of the Messiah (see Ps. 16; Isa. 53).

- Jesus predicted, on numerous occasions, His own death and resurrection (see Matt. 16:21).

- Jesus was betrayed by Judas; delivered to the chief priests for questioning; and interrogated, beaten and scourged by Pilate—as you may have seen in the movie *The Passion of the Christ* (see Matt. 26:57–27:31).

- The crowds cried for Jesus to be executed (see John 19:1-6).

- Jesus, according to Roman law, was nailed to a cross for crucifixion. The victim, weakened by the torture and loss of blood, was unable to lift his body into a position to take a breath and therefore died of suffocation (see Mark 15:20-41).

- A Roman executioner certified that Jesus was dead and put a spear through His chest cavity. Out of the wound flowed blood and water, indicating massive internal bleeding (see John 19:31-37).

- Jesus was anointed for burial and encased in more than 75 pounds of mummy-like wrappings (see John 19:38-42).

- Jesus' body was placed in a tomb, and a huge stone was rolled into place to block the entrance (see Mark 15:46).

- The tomb was sealed with a Roman seal, and a guard of Roman soldiers was placed in front of it (see Matt. 27:62-66).

- Three days later, the tomb was empty, and the stone had been moved a great distance away (see Mark 16:1-8).

- Jesus appeared on many occasions, and to many audiences, proving that He was alive. On one occasion, He appeared to more than 500 eyewitnesses simultaneously (see 1 Cor. 15:3-11).

- Jesus ascended bodily into heaven in the sight of the apostles (see Acts 1:9-11).

- The resurrected Jesus appeared to Saul of Tarsus, a Jewish Pharisee. Saul became a devout Christ-follower and an apostle, and his name was changed to Paul (see Acts 9).

- Bearing witness to Christ's resurrection transformed the lives of 12 fearful men, turning them into apostolic world-changers (see Acts 1–12).

- The resurrection of Jesus Christ is the foundation for the gospel that offers forgiveness of sins, new life and the hope of heaven (see 1 Cor. 15).

Either Jesus rose from the dead or He didn't. If He didn't, then there must be some other plausible explanation for the resurrection account. What are the possibilities? Here are four options that skeptics and others have presented:

1. *Jesus didn't really die.* Rather than dying on the cross, Jesus only passed out. In the dampness of the tomb, Jesus was revived and then appeared to the disciples, who mistakenly thought He was raised from the dead. This theory breaks down on several facts. First of all, crucifixions killed people! The victim literally suffocated to death. In Jesus' case, He was nailed to the cross, not merely tied down by ropes. A Roman executioner pierced His side with a sword, certifying His death. He was wrapped with about 75 pounds of ceremonial spices and linen wrappings. He was placed in a

tomb with a huge stone rolled across the entrance. A Roman guard was tasked with standing watch outside the tomb. Then, on multiple occasions over a 40-day period, He appeared to the disciples as the Lord of Life. Before a collective audience, He ascended out of their sight and into heaven. These facts, recorded by multiple eyewitnesses, refute the claim that Jesus didn't die.

2. *It wasn't Jesus on the cross.* A look-a-like took Jesus' place. The "resurrection" appearances were made by a perfectly healthy Jesus, who had never experienced the crucifixion and therefore didn't need to be raised from the dead. Again, this view has serious flaws. The foremost is that it would make Jesus a perpetrator of a lie. He would be some mastermind of a great religious deception. The apostles would also be liars. The Roman soldiers who experienced the miracle of the resurrection would be liars as well. This view disregards the evidence and accuracy of eyewitness testimony.

3. *The disciples stole the body, made up the story of the resurrection, and then preached it to others.* This view would have us believe that the disciples formed a huge religious plot. They somehow physically manhandled the Roman guard and then kept their secret to their deaths—martyrs' deaths. That's right—the disciples were killed for their faith. It's true that people have died for a lie, but it was a lie they believed was true. This theory asserts that the disciples propagated a lie and that they never denounced their lie, not even to save their own lives. Is it likely that not one person but many people, when faced with the option of freedom for telling the truth or torture and death for holding on to a lie, would continue to lie? The theory that the resurrection was a deceptive plot also breaks down when the case of the apostle Paul is considered. Paul claimed to have an

encounter with the resurrected Christ that was completely separate from the experiences of the other apostles. Based on this encounter, the entire direction of his life changed. If the disciples stole the body, then the conversion of the apostle Paul must be explained away.

4. *The resurrection accounts were hallucinations.* The apostles so wanted Jesus to be raised from the dead that they convinced themselves it had actually happened. This view does not fit the evidence: the empty tomb, the testimony of the Roman guard, and the fact that multiple people had the same "hallucination" on different occasions. In particular, the theory is hard-pressed to explain 500 people claiming to see the resurrected Jesus Christ. Again, the changed life of the apostle Paul discredits this interpretation.

Is there a view of the resurrection that fits all the facts? The obvious answer is yes. It is the view recorded by eyewitness testimony—the view that Jesus Christ bodily rose from the dead. This view is the very heart of the gospel; it is the view that we have already seen in 1 Corinthians 15. Let's revisit the opening of that passage:

> Now, brothers, I want to remind you of the gospel I preached to you, which you received and on which you have taken your stand. By this gospel you are saved, if you hold firmly to the word I preached to you. Otherwise, you have believed in vain. For what I received I passed on to you as of first importance: that Christ died for our sins according to the Scriptures, that he was buried, that he was raised on the third day according to the Scriptures, and that he appeared to Peter, and then to the Twelve. After that, he appeared to more than five hundred of the brothers at the same time, most of whom are still living, though some have fallen asleep. Then he appeared to James, then to all the apostles, and last of all he appeared to me also (1 Cor. 15:1-8).

The resurrection of Jesus Christ is a historical fact. It is backed up by prophetic prediction, eyewitness testimony, physical evidence and personal experience. It is the only conclusion that fits the evidence. *It is the resurrection of Jesus that validates His claim to be God and His assertion that He is able to forgive our sins and give us eternal life. And it is the resurrection of Jesus that defeats the Goliath of doubt.*

Doubt is going to taunt every man at one time or another. The answer to doubt is not to bury our heads in the sand. The answer to doubt is to appeal to the truth—especially the truth of Jesus Christ and His resurrection. Jesus said, "I am the way, and the truth, and the life: no one comes to the Father, but through Me" (John 14:6, *NASB*). When we put our focus on Jesus, God looks big and Goliath looks small.

Discussion

See It
Read 1 Samuel 17:1-11.

- Doubt can be a Goliath that stops a man in his tracks as he pursues after God. There can be nagging questions like: "Is God real?" "Why does God allow so much evil and suffering?" "With so many religions, how can Jesus be the only way to God?" "How do I really know that the Bible is true?" These questions, if left unchecked and unanswered, can grow into Goliath-sized doubts.

- How have you wrestled with the Goliath of doubt?

Discuss It
- Intellectual doubt is misplaced faith. It is faith based upon limited human perception, rather than faith based on who God is and what He has revealed in His Word.

- Read the following Scriptures and relate their truth to the intellectual doubt that can be a Goliath in a man's life. Remember, Jesus said that if we know the truth, the truth shall make us free!

- Isaiah 45:5-12; John 1:1-5; Colossians 1:15-20 (What is the truth found in these verses, and what doubt does this truth overcome?)

- Psalm 19:7-11; Matthew 5:17-19; 2 Timothy 3:16-17; 2 Peter 1:16-21 (What is the truth found in these verses, and what doubt does this truth overcome?)

- John 14:6; Acts 4:8-12; 1 Corinthians 15:1-4; Romans 10:9-10 (What is the truth found in these verses, and what doubt does this truth overcome?)

- John 3:16; Romans 5:8; Romans 8:28-39; 1 John 4:8-10 (What is the truth found in these verses, and what doubt does this truth overcome?)

Do It

To defeat the Goliath of doubt, we need to run to the truth, not away from it. What truth do you need to run to in order to defeat the Goliath of doubt in your life?

4

FACING THE GOLIATH OF FEAR

Franklin Delano Roosevelt said, "The only thing we have to fear is fear itself!" Fear is one of the biggest Goliaths that men face. The first wedding I ever officiated was of a good friend. While we were waiting for our time to enter the sanctuary, I asked the groom, "Why are you convinced you should get married?"

His deadpan answer broke up the whole wedding party: "Fear can be a powerful motivator!"

We can joke about the fear of a spouse, but real, gut-wrenching fear is no laughing matter. In fact, it's the stuff that causes a man to retreat into isolation, engage in an addiction, or hide in the darkness of guilt and shame. Fear is a significant obstacle to pursuing a relationship with Jesus Christ. It is a giant we must overcome in the Lord's strength.

Let's look again at 1 Samuel 17:8-11:

Goliath stood and shouted to the ranks of Israel, "Why do you come out and line up for battle? Am I not a Philistine, and are you not the servants of Saul? Choose a man and have him come down to me. If he is able to fight and kill me, we will become your subjects; but if I overcome him and kill him, you will become our subjects and serve us." Then the Philistine said, "This day I defy the ranks of Israel! Give me a man and let us fight each other." On hearing the Philistine's words, Saul and all the Israelites were dismayed and terrified.

What pitiful words: "Saul and all the Israelites were dismayed and terrified." The enemy's goal is to paralyze every us with fear. When we are afraid, we take our eyes off of God and put them on the object of our fear. When we are afraid, we become self-centered and defensive. When we are afraid, we lash out in anger and isolate ourselves in shame. When we are afraid, we become self-focused rather than God-focused—and we become vulnerable to Goliath-sized attacks. Weakened by fear, we become susceptible to temptation and deception, and we lose the spiritual battle.

Several years ago, I was praying with a group of men at a men's retreat for our church. The prayer coordinator asked us to confess any fears that held us back from fully trusting God. He directed us to name our fears and to speak them out loud—asking for Christ's healing and help. Rather than asking God to reveal any fears I struggled with, I immediately began to pray for the men gathered around me. I had never considered myself to be a person who struggled with fear, so I didn't feel I needed to pray about it. (This probably has to do with my struggle with pride, but we'll talk about that later!)

So, I sat there praying for others—and then all of a sudden, almost unconsciously, I found myself saying out loud, "I'm afraid . . . I'm afraid of failing." Wow! I almost panicked as I realized what I had just done. I mean, everyone had heard me. Now I really was afraid!

It was then that the Holy Spirit spoke to me in His still, small voice: *You are afraid of failing because you are really afraid that people won't love you if you fail.* With clarity, I reviewed my whole life: successful son, successful student, successful athlete, successful husband, successful dad, successful pastor. My life identity was about succeeding. My fear was that people loved me because I was a success. But what if I failed? Would people still love me?

At that prayer meeting, I came face to face with my fear of not being loved for who I am. I realized that under the surface, fear had been a motivator for much of what I did—even what I did as a Christ-follower. I realized that even many of the "spiritual" things that I did weren't done with totally pure motives. Somewhere in the mix, there was the desire to maintain an image: to look good, to be a pleaser. More than I wanted to admit, I was a poser because of fear.

Fear can paralyze us, and it can lead us to act in ways contrary to God's plan. Faith and fear cannot co-exist; they are like oil and water. Fear is a Goliath that every man must deal with at one time or another. Just as Goliath taunted the armies of Israel on that day thousands of years ago, fear continues to taunt each one of us today; and it had taunted men long before the days of David as well. One of the greatest heroes of the Bible—a powerful leader named Joshua—struggled with fear:

> After the death of Moses the servant of the LORD, the LORD said to Joshua son of Nun, Moses' aide: "Moses my servant is dead. Now then, you and all these people, get ready to cross the Jordan River into the land I am about to give to them—to the Israelites. I will give you every place where you set your foot, as I promised Moses. Your territory will extend from the desert to Lebanon, and from the great river, the Euphrates—all the Hittite country—to the Great Sea on the west. No one will be able to stand up against you all the days of your life. As I was with Moses, so I will be with you; I will never leave you nor forsake you.
>
> "Be strong and courageous, because you will lead these people to inherit the land I swore to their forefathers to give them. Be strong and very courageous. Be careful to obey all the law my servant Moses gave you; do not turn from it to the right or to the left, that you may be successful wherever you go. Do not let this Book of the Law depart from your mouth; meditate on it day and night, so that you may be careful to do everything written in it. Then you will be prosperous and successful. Have I not commanded you? Be strong and courageous. Do not be terrified; do not be discouraged, for the LORD your God will be with you wherever you go."
>
> So Joshua ordered the officers of the people: "Go through the camp and tell the people, 'Get your supplies

ready. Three days from now you will cross the Jordan here to go in and take possession of the land the LORD your God is giving you for your own'" (Josh. 1:1-11).

When Moses died, Joshua assumed command of the tribes of Israel. We see in this passage that as he began his leadership, God said to him, "Be strong and courageous. Be strong and courageous. Be strong and courageous." You don't have to be a Bible scholar to realize that if God says to someone three times, "Be strong and courageous," that person probably has a difficult time being strong and courageous!

Joshua was just like the rest of us. As my old football coach used to say, "He put his pants on one leg at a time." Even though he was one of the greatest military leaders of all time, he struggled with fear. Fear was a Goliath he had to face and defeat in God's strength.

In the movie *We Were Soldiers*, Mel Gibson plays the role of Vietnam War hero, Colonel Hal Moore. Colonel Moore commanded the Seventh Air Mobile Cavalry in the first major battle between American soldiers and the North Vietnamese Regular Army. As the movie unfolds, Colonel Moore and his troops are lured into an ambush in the Ian Drang Valley. Isolated from their base camp, they are surrounded and on the verge of being massacred. In the midst of the conflict, Moore has a desperate dialogue with his Sergeant Major, played by Sam Elliot. Moore confesses his fear that he has led his men to their deaths. As commander of the Seventh Cavalry, he says he feels like its infamous commander, George Armstrong Custer. At this statement, Sam Elliot, in full character, shoots back, "Custer was a p%##@ and you ain't no p%##@!" (Think of a term your football coach use to yell that speaks of being weak and wimpy.) *Satan's strategy is to make us feel emasculated as men.* He wants to exploit our fears, rob us of our identity and make us feel inadequate in our masculinity.

We saw, in 1 Samuel 17:11, that in response to Goliath's challenge, the men of Israel were "terrified and dismayed." These men were soldiers. They were challenged at the point of their deepest identity—and Goliath used fear to make them feel like total losers. Satan is the thief who comes to steal, kill and destroy. He uses fear to rob us of our manhood. He used fear on Joshua, and he will use fear on us.

There is an important truth to be learned from Joshua: *Courage is not the absence of fear; courage is trusting God in spite of our fears.* As long as we are in these sin-affected bodies, we will have to deal with fear. Only in heaven will all fear be removed. But fear can be faced—by trusting God. Courage is looking to God rather than Goliath—the source of our fears. Courage believes what God says rather than the lies of the enemy. Courage is honestly acknowledging that we are afraid and asking for God's help and support. Courage is inviting some trusted brothers into our lives and leaning on their strength. I repeat: *Courage is looking to God rather than Goliath.*

Joshua was given one of the greatest responsibilities possible: to lead a mobile army, along with their families, across the barren desert into the Promised Land. Many Bible scholars estimate the number of men, women and children at 2 to 3 million! Once in this new land, Joshua was to face and defeat enemy nations, set up a new government, and rule his people. No simple task. Of course he was afraid. Fear can be a Goliath that defeats us, or it can give us an opportunity to trust God and see His power released in our lives. God's word to Joshua is His word to us: "Be strong and courageous!"

Joshua understood fear and the need to be strong in the Lord. From his example, we can learn how to defeat this Goliath in our lives. To defeat the Goliath of fear, we must be strong in God's promises. God promised Joshua several things: He promised that Joshua and the Israelites would cross the Jordan and receive the land He had said He would give to them. He promised that He would give them every place they set their feet. He promised the precise boundaries of the land He was going to give them. God promised Joshua that no one would be able to stand up against him all the days of his life. Best of all, He promised to be with him all the days of his life. God promised that He would never leave nor forsake Joshua (see Josh. 1:2-5).

That's like learning before you play the championship football game that you are going to be victorious, be uninjured, and have the game of your life. If you know the outcome with certainty and believe it, even if your opponent scores or you miss a tackle, you will have confidence because you are assured of the final victory. You can shake off a temporary bump and bruise, get back up, and give it 110 percent—because you have the confidence that you will ultimately be the winner.

During my son's senior year, his high school football team won the league championship and continued to play in the county playoffs. In their second game of the playoffs, they were matched up against a team with an explosive offense. At halftime, the score was 34-7 in their opponents' favor. Now, I know it ain't over 'til the fat lady sings, but I really believed there was no way my son's team was going to come back and win the game. Emotionally, this season was a big deal—for me as well as for my son. Not only was I proud of him, but this year also brought back all the great memories I had of playing high school football myself. So at halftime, on that Friday night, I was a wreck—because I had convinced myself the season was over. You see, I was looking at the game from my vantage point. I couldn't see the end from the beginning. What happened in the second half of the game was amazing. My son's team came back and played with reckless abandon—and they won the game, 54-48! If I had known the final outcome ahead of time, do you think I would have been an emotional mess at halftime? No way! I would have been confident in the final victory.

God gives us promises so that we can be confident in His final victory. Joshua was about to embark on the biggest challenge of his life, and he was afraid. Goliath was looking large. God said, "Be strong and courageous in My promises." What promises has God given to you to help you face the Goliath of fear?

The Bible is filled with promises that you and I can bank on. When we write checks, we understand that a withdrawal is going to be made on our checking account. If our withdrawals exceed our deposits, we are overdrawn. We could decide we would like to purchase a new car, a new home or a dream vacation, but if we don't have the money in our account, our checks are just going to bounce. The purchases would seem great at the time, but they would not be realistic—and things would not go well for us in the long run. Many men feel that way about living the Christian life. The commands of Jesus, the challenges of being the spiritual leaders of their families, and a life of personal victory sound awesome, but most men are afraid they don't have what it takes to follow Christ for the long haul. Maybe that's the way you feel: to even try will leave you with an overdrawn spiritual account!

Now, to stick with the banking illustration for just a little longer, if you had a deposit slip showing that a hundred million dollars had been put into your account, don't you think you would have more confidence to make those purchases? You would know that you had all the funds you needed to buy whatever you wanted. The promises of God are like that deposit slip. They are God's guarantee that we have all the resources we need in order to respond to God's call. God's promises tell us of His provision to carry out His will for our lives:

> His divine power has given us everything we need for life and godliness through our knowledge of him who called us by his own glory and goodness. Through these he has given us his very great and precious promises, so that through them you may participate in the divine nature and escape the corruption in the world caused by evil desires (2 Pet. 1:3-4).

Like Joshua, we have promises from God to give us strength and courage. These promises are power punches, aimed right at the enemy's midsection, that cause him to double over in defeat. A few years ago, I attended the first Ultimate Fighting Championship bout at the Arrowhead Pond in Anaheim, California. The stadium was packed with 20,000 testosterone-filled fans cheering on the mixed martial arts competition—and those were just the women! The heavyweight championship fight turned out to be a good old-fashioned boxing match. The winner, Tim Sylvia, used a combination of rights and lefts to defeat his opponent. Claiming God's promises is like launching a barrage of rights and lefts at the Goliath of fear. We are not victims. We are not helpless in the spiritual battle. According to James 4:7, we can resist the devil—and he will flee from us!

Here are just a few of the amazing promises you can claim in order to defeat the Goliath of fear:

> So do not fear, for I am with you; do not be dismayed, for I am your God. I will strengthen you and help you; I will uphold you with my righteous right hand (Isa. 41:10).

> Do not be anxious about anything, but in everything, by prayer and petition, with thanksgiving, present your requests to God. And the peace of God, which transcends all understanding, will guard your hearts and your minds in Christ Jesus (Phil. 4:6-7).

> For God did not give us a spirit of timidity, but a spirit of power, of love and of self-discipline (2 Tim. 1:7).

> Submit yourselves, then, to God. Resist the devil, and he will flee from you (Jas. 4:7).

When we claim these promises, it's like when the Scarecrow threw water on the Wicked Witch in *The Wizard of Oz*. Remember her response: "I'm melting!" Fear melts away when doused with faith in the promises of God.

Every man faces the Goliath of fear. Fear can paralyze us; it can emasculate us and rob us of our identity in Christ. When we face the Goliath of fear by putting our faith in the promises of God, then God looks big and Goliath looks small.

Discussion

See It
Read 1 Samuel 17:1-11,16,24.

- Why do you think the Israelites were filled with fear when they saw and heard Goliath?

• How is fear a Goliath that can stop a man from pursuing a relationship with Christ?

Discuss It

• Goliath-induced fear is a result of believing a lie. What kind of lies do men believe that cause them to see God as small and Goliath as big?

• Joshua was a man who understood fear. Read Joshua 1:1-11. What exhortation does God repeat to Joshua?

• Based on God's promise, what was to be Joshua's source of courage in the face of his fears?

• How can a man put his eyes on God and trust in His promises rather than succumb to his fears?

Do It

• What attributes and promises of God do you need to believe in order to combat your fears?

• Read Joshua 1:1-11 again. How can you be strong and courageous?

5

FACING THE GOLIATH
OF PRIDE

"Vanity, definitely my favorite sin." This is the closing line from the movie *The Devil's Advocate,* starring Al Pacino and Keanu Reeves. In this film, Keanu Reeves plays Kevin Lomax, a hotshot southern attorney who has never lost a case. Al Pacino plays John Milton, a high-powered New York lawyer who hires Lomax for his firm. The movie opens with a courtroom scene in which Lomax is defending a man accused of child molestation. Even though he finds out at the last minute that his client is guilty, Lomax's desire to win the case causes him to defend his client to an acquittal. After this victory, Milton offers Lomax a job and all the glamour that goes along with it.

Through a series of intense and graphic scenes, Lomax comes to realize that Milton is really the devil—and his intention is to seduce Lomax and capture his soul. In a final moment of defiance and desperation, Lomax fights back and resists Milton's temptation. At this point, in a cinematic moment, Lomax returns to the courthouse scene that opened the movie. He is back to the instant when he first learned that his client was actually guilty of child molestation.

With clarity and conviction, Lomax goes back into court, divulges the information of his client's guilt, and excuses himself from his defense. As he is walking out of the courtroom, a reporter stops him with a barrage of questions. The reporter tells Lomax that he is going to be on *60 Minutes*, and that he is going to be famous. After thinking about it for a moment, Lomax agrees, somewhat smugly, to an interview. As he walks away, the reporter morphs into John Milton as the devil, who says, "Vanity, definitely my favorite sin."

When I first saw *The Devil's Advocate*, I thought, *This is precisely how Satan operates!* Pride is one of the biggest Goliaths that men face. Pride seduces, pride deceives, and pride can take us down.

When we are prideful, we dethrone Christ from His rightful place in our lives and put self in charge. Consumed with self, we bully, we feel entitled, we act passive-aggressively, we become stubborn, and we stifle the flow of God's grace into our lives. James explains:

> But he gives us more grace. That is why Scripture says: "God opposes the proud but gives grace to the humble." Submit yourselves, then, to God. Resist the devil, and he will flee from you (Jas. 4:6-7).

When we are prideful, we make ourselves God's opponents. I may not be the sharpest tool in the shed, but I know that if a man is fighting against God, he is going to lose! Pride and grace cannot co-exist. Grace flows into our lives when we are humble; when we are prideful, our hearts become hard, and we shut off the grace we need to resist the devil. Pride and the devil go hand in hand. That is why pride is a huge Goliath for every man.

The devil's relationship to pride is well documented. The prophet Isaiah gives us an allegorical description of Satan and his rebellion against God:

> How you have fallen from heaven, O morning star, son of the dawn! You have been cast down to the earth, you who once laid low the nations! You said in your heart, "I will ascend to heaven; I will raise my throne above the stars of God; I will sit enthroned on the mount of assembly, on the utmost heights of the sacred mountain. I will ascend above the tops of the clouds; I will make myself like the Most High." But you are brought down to the grave, to the depths of the pit (Isa. 14:12-15).

This passage references "the morning star, the son of the dawn." In Hebrew, the word is *heylel*. When the Hebrew Bible was translated into Latin, the term became *Lucifer*. Because of the influence of the Latin Bible, Lucifer was adopted into church vocabulary as a name for Satan. Satan is described in this passage as being judged because he asserted his will over against God's.

Notice Lucifer's statements: "I will ascend to heaven; I will raise my throne above the stars of God; I will sit enthroned on the mount of assembly, on the utmost heights of the sacred mountain. I will ascend above the tops of the clouds; I will make myself like the Most High." Satan was consumed with himself. Pride caused him to rebel against God, and pride was the basis for God's judgment upon him. Proverbs 16:18 warns, "Pride goes before destruction, a haughty spirit before a fall." Satan's pride is the prototype for all prideful action.

When David stepped into the Valley of Elah, he had humble confidence in the Lord's victory. Goliath, full of pride and arrogance, taunted the man of God. Pride will taunt us, deceive us, and seek to rule us. The Bible is full of warnings against pride. In particular, a number of warnings are found in the book of Proverbs. Proverbs is a series of wise sayings that give practical advice on how to live a godly life. Because pride is a constant Goliath, many of the sayings in this book address this enemy:

> There are six things the LORD hates, seven that are detestable to him: haughty eyes, a lying tongue, hands that shed innocent blood (Prov. 6:16-17).

> To fear the LORD is to hate evil; I hate pride and arrogance, evil behavior and perverse speech (Prov. 8:13).

> When pride comes, then comes disgrace, but with humility comes wisdom (Prov. 11:2).

> Pride only breeds quarrels, but wisdom is found in those who take advice (Prov. 13:10).

> Pride goes before destruction, a haughty spirit before a fall (Prov. 16:18).

Haughty eyes and a proud heart, the lamp of the wicked, are sin! (Prov. 21:4).

The proud and arrogant man—"Mocker" is his name; he behaves with overweening pride (Prov. 21:24).

A man's pride brings him low, but a man of lowly spirit gains honor (Prov. 29:23).

Several years ago, my wife and I were attending a worship service together. The speaker was describing a serious conversation he had had with his wife. During a moment of brutal honesty, his wife had said that she thought he acted with real selfishness. Listening intently, I looked over at my wife and asked, "Honey, do you think I am selfish?"

My wife smiled back at me and said, "No, I would have to say that you are not selfish . . . you are the most prideful person I have ever met, but you are not selfish." Talk about conviction! My wife had nailed it. I struggled with the Goliath of pride—and, more often than I cared to admit, Goliath had won.

Often the real issue in a man's refusal to repent and believe in Christ is pride. Jesus said:

I tell you the truth, unless you change and become like little children, you will never enter the kingdom of heaven. Therefore, whoever humbles himself like this child is the greatest in the kingdom of heaven (Matt. 18:3-4).

Coming to Christ is a pride-crushing experience. We must humble ourselves before God, acknowledge that we cannot save ourselves, and ask Jesus Christ to be our Lord and Savior. Years ago, I was part of a Christian sports ministry called American Football Ministries International. We used the platform of American football to take the gospel to Eastern Europe and the former Soviet Union. On one summer missions experience, we played against a Russian team made up of athletes from different sports. The starting full-back for the Russian team was a man named Oleg. Oleg had been in the Russian Special Forces and had been bayoneted in combat in Afghanistan. He had a big scar on his chest from the wound he had received right before he knocked the rifle and bayonet away and then killed his attacker. Yeah, that's right, I played football against this guy!

My position that summer was inside linebacker, so on dive plays up the middle, it was me against Oleg. A linebacker can miss the tackle in two ways on this kind of play: He can overcommit himself and get caught up in the line of scrimmage, or the linebacker can dance around, play it safe, and get juked by the ball carrier as he runs past him. The only way to make a sure tackle is to break down, step up and meet the ball carrier head on, and absorb the full contact. Believe me, this can be bone-crushing.

Similarly, when a man considers the call of Jesus Christ in the gospel, he has three choices: He can overcommit and get involved in the trappings of religion—majoring on the minors and missing Jesus Christ completely. A second possible response is to stay back, defer making a decision, and passively take himself out of encountering Christ. The man's third option—and the only way he can have a life-changing experience with Christ—is to meet Christ head-on: to believe the gospel, receive Christ, and personally ask Him to be the Lord of his life. This kind of commitment is pride-crushing. It requires the believer to surrender his whole life to Christ.

For some men, the Goliath of pride is so strong in their lives that they stubbornly refuse to surrender to Christ. The Pharisees of Jesus' day were men like this. They had the opportunity to hear Jesus, see His miracles, and check His claims against the authority of Scripture—yet they continued in their unbelief. The Goliath of pride clouded their judgment and hardened their hearts. Jesus addressed this kind of pride specifically:

> If I testify about myself, my testimony is not valid. There is another who testifies in my favor, and I know that his testimony about me is valid.

You have sent to John and he has testified to the truth. Not that I accept human testimony; but I mention it that you may be saved. John was a lamp that burned and gave light, and you chose for a time to enjoy his light.

I have testimony weightier than that of John. For the very work that the Father has given me to finish, and which I am doing, testifies that the Father has sent me. And the Father who sent me has himself testified concerning me. You have never heard his voice nor seen his form, nor does his word dwell in you, for you do not believe the one he sent. You diligently study the Scriptures because you think that by them you possess eternal life. These are the Scriptures that testify about me, yet you refuse to come to me to have life.

I do not accept praise from men, but I know you. I know that you do not have the love of God in your hearts. I have come in my Father's name, and you do not accept me; but if someone else comes in his own name, you will accept him. How can you believe if you accept praise from one another, yet make no effort to obtain the praise that comes from the only God?

But do not think I will accuse you before the Father. Your accuser is Moses, on whom your hopes are set. If you believed Moses, you would believe me, for he wrote about me. But since you do not believe what he wrote, how are you going to believe what I say? (John 5:31-47).

Like an attorney arguing before a jury, Jesus presents His case to the Pharisees—proving that He is the Messiah and the Son of God by appealing to the testimony of His own words, the testimony of John the Baptist, the testimony of His miracles, the testimony of the Father's voice, the testimony of the Scriptures, and the testimony of Moses. The problem with the Pharisees, Jesus says, is not a lack of testimony but an unwillingness to surrender to God—a prideful concern for their own reputation rather than a seeking of God's praise. In verses 41-44, He nails it:

I do not accept praise from men, but I know you. I know that you do not have the love of God in your hearts. I have come in my Father's name, and you do not accept me; but if someone else comes in his own name, you will accept him. How can you believe if you accept praise from one another, yet make no effort to obtain the praise that comes from the only God?

Some men will not believe because their pride stands in the way. What about you? Are you letting pride stop you from repenting and believing in Christ? Don't let the Goliath of pride rob you of salvation. Humble yourself before God. Ask Jesus Christ to save you. Surrender yourself to Christ's lordship and let Jesus defeat the Goliath of pride.

If Goliath cannot stop a man from receiving salvation, he will seek to rob that man of his God-ordained identity and call. Pride confronts us in our journey both before and after we give our lives to Christ. Writing about the qualifications for spiritual leadership, Paul warned Timothy:

Here is a trustworthy saying: If anyone sets his heart on being an overseer, he desires a noble task. . . . He must not be a recent convert, or he may become conceited and fall under the same judgment as the devil (1 Tim. 3:1-6).

Spiritual leaders are to be men who, because of maturity, are able to avoid the pitfall of conceit. Young believers are particularly vulnerable to this Goliath. Full of energy and passion, they can easily become ego-invested in Kingdom work. Losing sight of the fact that they are servants of the King, they may become defensive to criticism and seek to control others. The Goliath of pride is not always so obvious, but it is always an offense to the glory of God.

Religious pride is the worst. Statements like, "Buy my next book, *The Ten Most Humble Men in the World and How I Discipled the Other Nine*," are way too common in church circles. Years ago, I was on a mission's project in Hawaii doing beach evangelism. I know, tough assignment. My job was to train college students in personal evangelism, and the crowded beach was a natural laboratory in which to practice what we were learning. One young man in the group was very gifted but struggled with what I will call "reverse pride." He went out of his way to put himself down, so that even though he was being self-deprecating, he was still talking about himself! You know the old line: "Enough about me, let's talk about you—what do you think of me?"

After an evening outreach where the young man spoke and shared his testimony in Christ, I complimented him by saying he had done a great job.

"No, no, it wasn't me. It was all Jesus," was the young man's response.

I looked at him and softly but directly said, "Well, if it was all Jesus, it would have been a lot better, but you did a good job. Thanks." Humility is not putting ourselves down; it is lifting Jesus and others up.

Pride is such a deceiver. Many men see the pride in others but cannot recognize it in themselves. Jeff Foxworthy, the blue-collar comedian, became famous with his "You may be a redneck if . . ." jokes. In order to check your own heart to see if the Goliath of pride is getting the better of you, personally consider the following:

1. You may be being defeated by the Goliath of pride if you have never surrendered your life to Jesus Christ.

2. You may be being defeated by the Goliath of pride if your first response to this chapter is to defend yourself.

3. You may be being defeated by the Goliath of pride if you think about how others need to apply these truths, but you don't think about your own application.

4. You may be being defeated by the Goliath of pride if you have been stuck in the same place in your spiritual journey for a long time.

5. You may be being defeated by the Goliath of pride if you are a poser, a fake or a hypocrite.

If pride is kicking your butt, destroying your relationships, and standing as a Goliath between you and God, then meet him head-on in face-to-face combat.

Humility is the only way to deal with the Goliath of pride. Both in coming to Christ for salvation and in following Christ in discipleship, the key is humility. When we get ourselves out of the way, Jesus is glorified as the only one who can transform our lives and defeat our Goliaths. But knowing this and doing it are two different things. The pathway to humble repentance is brutal. In his epistle, James describes the Goliath of pride and the hard path of humility:

> What causes fights and quarrels among you? Don't they come from your desires that battle within you? You want something but don't get it. You kill and covet, but you cannot have what you want. You quarrel and fight. You do not have, because you do not ask God. When you ask, you do not receive, because you ask with wrong motives, that you may spend what you get on your pleasures.
>
> You adulterous people, don't you know that friendship with the world is hatred toward God? Anyone who chooses to be a friend of the world becomes an enemy of God. Or do you think Scripture says without reason that the spirit he caused to live in us envies intensely? But he gives us more grace. That is why Scripture says: "God opposes the proud but gives grace to the humble."
>
> Submit yourselves, then, to God. Resist the devil, and he will flee from you. Come near to God and he will come near to you. Wash your hands, you sinners, and purify your hearts, you double-minded. Grieve, mourn and wail. Change your laughter to mourning and your joy to gloom. Humble yourselves before the Lord, and he will lift you up (Jas. 4:1-10).

We fight, we desire, we covet, and we wrestle with the world—all because of pride. Even when we seek God, often our pursuit is motivated by pride. Loving the world and loving God cannot co-exist. The man who would experience Christ's victory over his Goliath must crucify pride and walk the path of humility. God gives us the grace to do what is difficult. So, we are commanded to submit ourselves to God; resist the devil; come near to God; wash our hands and purify our hearts from sin; grieve, mourn, wail and repent; and humble ourselves before the Lord (giving Him the opportunity to lift us up). This is quite a list! Humility is a commitment. It involves repentance, submission, cleansing, and a determination to resist the devil. We cannot do these things on our own. It is only by the grace of God that we can seek Him and obey His commandments.

Our part is to humble ourselves before the Lord. God's part is to give us His grace. Our part is to receive His grace and put it into practice. God's part is to give us victory. Our part is to trust the Lord. God's part is to defeat Goliath. When we walk in humility, we can face the Goliath of pride.

Discussion

See It
Read 1 Samuel 17:1-11,16,24.
- Goliaths intimidate, paralyze and defeat us. Why do you think it is important for men to accurately understand the nature of the Goliaths they face?

- One of the Goliaths that will stand in the way of our spiritual growth is pride. How do you think pride can rob a man of pursuing the knowledge of Christ and the love of God?

Discuss It
- Look up the following verses and discuss the nature, symptoms and consequences of pride: Proverbs 13:10; Proverbs 16:18; John 5:39-44; Matthew 23:1-12; Romans 2:1-6.

- The prideful man is addicted to defending and controlling. What effect can this have on a marriage, a family, or a working relationship?

- Look up James 4:6-7. If a man gives in to the Goliath of pride, what is inevitable in terms of his relationship with Christ?

Do It

- According to James 4:6-10 and Mark 10:42-45, what must a man be willing to do if he is going to conquer the Goliath of pride?

- How will you humble yourself before the Lord in order to receive His grace and help in combating pride?

FACING THE GOLIATH
OF LUST

David, the man of God, won his battle against the human Goliath but lost his battle against the Goliath of lust. In 1 Samuel 17, we read about how David stepped into the Valley of Elah and faced Goliath. With unshakeable confidence in God, he ran to battle and defeated his enemy. As a result of this great feat, David immediately earned a reputation:

> When the men were returning home after David had killed the Philistine, the women came out from all the towns of Israel to meet King Saul with singing and dancing, with joyful songs and with tambourines and lutes. As they danced, they sang: "Saul has slain his thousands, and David his tens of thousands" (1 Sam. 18:6-7).

David was a warrior, a victor and a giant-killer. But, to use the common vernacular, he couldn't keep it in his pants.

David was a man of passion. He was passionate for God, passionate as a leader, and passionate as a man with sexual desire. David's downfall is recorded for us in 2 Samuel 11:1-5:

> In the spring, at the time when kings go off to war, David sent Joab out with the king's men and the whole Israelite army. They destroyed the Ammonites and besieged Rabbah. But David remained in Jerusalem. One evening David got up from his bed and walked around on the roof of the palace. From the roof he saw a woman bathing. The woman

was very beautiful, and David sent someone to find out about her. The man said, "Isn't this Bathsheba, the daughter of Eliam and the wife of Uriah the Hittite?" Then David sent messengers to get her. She came to him, and he slept with her. (She had purified herself from her uncleanness.) Then she went back home. The woman conceived and sent word to David, saying, "I am pregnant."

Let's review. David was out on his balcony, and he noticed a beautiful woman taking a bath. He was attracted to her, so he inquired about who she was. He found out about the woman—who happened to be married to one of his soldiers—sent for her, and slept with her. A while later, he found out that his sexual liaison had resulted in her pregnancy. David, the man of God, committed adultery and then launched into a downward spiritual spiral of lies, cover-up and murder.

What happened between 1 Samuel 17 and 2 Samuel 11? How did the giant-killer become the adulterer? Answering these questions is crucial, because every one of us could go down the path of David. Lust is a Goliath we must face and defeat if we are going to follow after Jesus Christ. Many a good man has stumbled and never recovered from the attack of this enemy. David's example helps us understand what makes us vulnerable to the Goliath of lust.

We are vulnerable to the Goliath of lust when we take a break from fighting the battle. "In the spring, at the time when kings go off to war, David sent Joab out with the king's men and the whole Israelite army. They destroyed the Ammonites and besieged Rabbah. But David remained in Jerusalem" (2 Sam. 11:1). It was the time of year when kings went off to war. In the past, David was on the front lines, leading the charge. He suited up and said, "Follow me." But not this time. David stayed in Jerusalem and sent Joab to lead the troops in his place. David was taking a break from the fight. When we take a break from the fight, we are vulnerable. We lose our edge and our defenses are down. In Jerusalem, David was more vulnerable to lust than he would have been had he joined his men in the fight.

Sometimes we get tired of fighting the spiritual battle. We reason that we need a break. But our enemy knows our weaknesses. When we let down our guard, he is right there with a flaming missile to assault us. When we are passive or lazy, or when we spiritually check out, we are vulnerable to the Goliath of lust. As James explains:

> When tempted, no one should say, "God is tempting me." For God cannot be tempted by evil, nor does he tempt anyone; but each one is tempted when, by his own evil desire, he is dragged away and enticed. Then, after desire has conceived, it gives birth to sin; and sin, when it is full-grown, gives birth to death (Jas. 1:13-15).

Temptation comes from our desire within us. If we give in to our lusts and act on our temptation, then we sin—and sin leads to death. Emotionally disengaging from the battle does not remove us from the assault of lust. In fact, it only intensifies it. We take our lusts with us, because they come from our internal desires. The term "lust" is the English translation of the Greek word *epithumia*, which means a strong, passionate desire. We can have a lust for righteousness or a lust for worshiping God. Desires are good; it is what we do with our desires that determines whether they move us toward obedient seeking of Christ or lustful indulgence. When a man removes himself from the battle, he loses the context that reminds him that he is fighting evil. He is without accountability, and his desires become perverted. To quote from *The Fellowship of the Ring*, "The hearts of men are easily corrupted." Lust becomes a temptation, temptation becomes an act of sin, and sin leads to death.

If you are seeking to avoid all spiritual conflict, your passivity could be your downfall. Removed from the battle, you will make subtle compromises. Lust will become a seed that, if not uprooted, will bear the fruit of sin. Learn from the example of David. Be proactively engaged in seeking after Christ and fighting the spiritual battle. If you are intentional about fighting the fight, your forward progress will minimize the onslaught of lust.

We are vulnerable to the Goliath of lust when we are at the wrong place at the wrong time. Rather than being at the front lines of the battle, David was walking around his balcony at the palace. Here is a simple question: "Are we more vulnerable to the Goliath of lust sitting in church at 11:00 AM on Sunday or sitting in a singles bar at 1:00 AM on a Saturday night?" For the godly man, some places are just off limits. For the godly man, some pursuits and practices are unwise and unprofitable in the quest to become more like Jesus Christ.

I recently had a conversation with a young man who had a history of alcohol addiction. He was thinking about the potential harm of having a social drink and was reasoning that he could handle it without a problem. Let me say here that I don't think the Bible teaches across-the-board abstinence in drinking. The warnings in Scripture are about drunkenness—not the occasional enjoyment of an adult beverage. Having said that, let me also say that I have seen nothing but destruction in the lives of abusers and their victims when it comes to overindulgence of alcohol. Alcoholism is a disease and a behavior that devastates the lives of many. As this young man discussed with me his thoughts, I posed the following story to him as a way of challenging his thinking:

A man owned a glass manufacturing business that sold its products to a neighboring town. The town was on the other side of a mountain that could only be crossed by way of a narrow and winding one-lane road. The business owner needed to hire a van driver who would make daily deliveries of his glass products. He interviewed two candidates for the job.

After some initial questions, he asked the first applicant, "How close to the edge of the cliff do you think you could drive without falling off?"

The applicant thought and responded confidently, "I am an expert driver, and I feel certain that I could drive within six inches of the cliff and still maintain the speed limit in driving through the pass."

The owner thanked the applicant and interviewed the second person. Again after a few questions, he asked, "How close to the edge of the cliff do you think you could drive without falling off?"

The young applicant nodded his head that he understood the question. Then he responded, "Well, I am sure I could drive very close, but if you hire me, I will do my best to drive close to the mountain and as far away from the edge as I can."

The owner extended his hand and said, "You're hired."

For the man who struggles with the Goliath of lust, the question should never be: "What kind of situations can I put myself in to test my self-control?" The wise man will avoid experiences that will obviously invite lustful temptation. David was in the wrong place at the wrong time. He underestimated his enemy and over-estimated his own resolve to resist. In the words of the great theologian Clint Eastwood, from the movie *Magnum Force*, "A man's got to know his limitations."

A third situation that makes us vulnerable to the Goliath of lust is when we are looking. David was walking around his balcony rather than leading the charge in battle. While looking over the rooftops of Jerusalem, he noticed a young woman taking a bath. In ancient times, water was stored on rooftops. In was not uncommon for a person to be bathing on the roof. This was in the evening; Bathsheba was being modest and thinking she would be unnoticed. But David spotted her. He watched her. He fantasized about her. He stalked her.

After our high school graduation, my best friends and I went on a camping trip on the Yuba River in Northern California. We were five guys hanging out, fishing and canoeing down the river. Unbeknownst to us, there was a hippie commune back in the woods, not far from where we were camping. One day we decided to hike along the river—and we abruptly barged into several naked people frolicking in the water. Now, immediately I noticed the naked women. Without inhibition, they waved and invited us into the water. Whether it was youthful embarrassment or God's protection, all of us averted our eyes, turned around, and walked the other way. We were guys, so of course we noticed the women—but we didn't stare or gawk. We ran away!

When a man is looking for sin, he finds it. When a man is looking for an outlet for his lustful passion, it becomes available. When a man has already determined that he is going to give in to lust, he does. When we are looking, sin is always found. God's words to Cain apply to every man: "Why are you angry? Why is your face downcast? If you do what is right, will you not be accepted? But if you do not do what is right, sin is crouching at your door; it desires to have you, but you must master it" (Gen. 4:6-7). The Goliath of lust is crouching at the door. We must master it and defeat it.

We are vulnerable to the Goliath of lust when we are not accountable. Rather than being with his men, David was alone in the palace. His servants, intimidated by his authority, lacked the freedom to speak truth into his life. With no accountability, David was left to his own devices and gave in to temptation. When we are alone, and no one knows what we are doing, the Goliath of lust attacks us. When we are without accountability, we become deceived and believe the lies of the enemy.

Several years ago, my family lived in Thousand Oaks, California. I was the senior pastor of a local church and used to study for my sermons on the patio of a Starbucks coffee shop. The patio was part of a larger outdoor mall, and many folks would sit outside and enjoy the Southern California weather. One day I had my coffee, my Bible and several commentaries stacked on the table in front of me. Engrossed in my study, I tuned out all the chatter and outdoor noise.

Then, in my peripheral vision, I noticed an attractive woman with blonde hair smiling and looking in my direction. I looked up and returned the smile. I thought to myself that she was probably someone who had visited my church or someone I had met in the community. As I started to look back down to my sermon notes, I realized that she had gotten up and was walking my way. I turned my head and smiled again as she walked over to my table. To be honest, in the time she walked toward me, I saw that she possessed many physical qualities men find attractive and alluring (yes, I am a man, and I noticed!). When she got to my table, she said, "Hi, I have seen you here before."

I replied that I came here a lot; I liked the coffee and it was a good place to study.

She then said, "I told my friend that there was the guy I had seen before on the patio." I looked past her, and her friend was waving at me, so I waved back. The woman continued, "I asked my friend what should I say to him, and she said, 'Why don't you just say, "Here I am. Take me; I'm yours"?' So, here I am. Take me; I'm yours!"

I immediately felt hot all over, and I am sure I began to sweat. *Oh my gosh, this woman is trying to pick me up!* a panicked voice screamed inside my head.

Before I could stammer out a response, she looked at my hand and asked, "Is that a ring? Are you married?"

"Yes and yes," I said.

"Is that a Bible?" she practically shouted.

"It gets worse," I said. "I am a pastor."

"Oh no, I tried to pick up the pastor," she wailed. After she calmed down, she tried to tell me that she had never done that before and was ashamed of herself.

I thanked her for the compliment of being attracted to me and encouraged her to attend another church in town (not mine!). After she left, I gathered up my things and got into my car. I immediately phoned my wife and told her everything that had happened. I wanted my wife to pray for me and to hold me accountable. I knew that even though I had resisted temptation in that moment, the evil one would bring the incident back in my thoughts—and very likely bring that woman back into my life. I wanted accountability to continue to stay on the right path.

A few weeks later, my wife and I were on a date and walked into a local restaurant. As we were walking in, the temptress from the patio was walking out. We smiled and said hello as she walked past us; then my wife gripped my arm and said, "That's her, isn't it?" Accountability is always our friend to help us resist the Goliath of lust. The writer of Hebrews exhorts us, "See to it, brothers, that none of you has a sinful, unbelieving heart that turns away from the living God. But encourage one another daily, as long as it is called Today, so that none of you may be hardened by sin's deceitfulness" (Heb. 3:12-13). Every man needs the encouragement and accountability of others so that he does not become hardened by the deceitfulness of sin. When we are not accountable, we are vulnerable to the Goliath of lust.

A final factor that makes us vulnerable to the Goliath of lust is when we do not immediately yield our temptation to Christ. David was not where he was supposed to be. He was up on the balcony, looking for an opportunity to sin. He saw Bathsheba, and his lusts were activated with temptation. At that point, David had a choice: give in to temptation and act out in sin, or yield his temptation to God and ask for His help. Every man faces this same choice when the Goliath of lust attacks. Sin is always a choice. The apostle Paul promises:

> No temptation has seized you except what is common to man. And God is faithful; he will not let you be tempted beyond what you can bear. But when you are tempted, he will also provide a way out so that you can stand up under it (1 Cor. 10:13).

God provides a way of escape from every temptation. Even when Bathsheba was lying naked on the bed in front of David, he still could have resisted consummating the act. However, his righteous resolve was much stronger when he first noticed her on the balcony. As I often say when speaking to youth, "You should determine your convictions long before the windows are fogged up in the car!" The more we give sin an opportunity to establish a foothold in our heart and mind, the more likely we are to fully give in to it.

Every temptation should be immediately surrendered to Jesus Christ. When we ask for His help, He is faithful and responsive:

> Therefore, since we have a great high priest who has gone through the heavens, Jesus the Son of God, let us hold firmly to the faith we profess. For we do not have a high priest who is unable to sympathize with our weaknesses, but we have one who has been tempted in every way, just as we are—yet was without sin. Let us then approach the throne of grace with confidence, so that we may receive mercy and find grace to help us in our time of need (Heb. 4:14-16).

When the Goliath of lust invades our lives, we can ask for the help of Jesus to resist temptation and walk in victory. He understands and sympathizes with our weaknesses, and He is faithful to give us grace and help in our time of need.

Recognizing when we are vulnerable is one aspect of the ongoing fight against the Goliath of lust. In order to face Goliath and defeat him, we also need a positive biblical game plan. Several Scriptures, taken together, give us a holistic strategy for facing the Goliath of lust. The first is Galatians 5:16: "But I say, walk by the Spirit, and you will not carry out the desire of the flesh" (*NASB*). When we walk by the Spirit, we will not carry out the desires of the flesh. The text does not say we won't *have* the desires of the flesh. If you are praying that God would take away your desires, you might as well stop. The key is not to divest yourself of your desires; it is to surrender your desires to the control of the Holy Spirit. When the Holy Spirit is in control of our lives, we don't act out and lustfully fulfill our desires. The term translated as "carry out" in this verse is the Greek word *teleo*.

Teleo means to bring to an end, to complete, to finish or to carry out. Walking by the Spirit ensures that we do not follow through on our desires by engaging in lustful and sinful acts. The temptation may be present, but we resist it and choose the way of escape that Christ provides. Walking by the Spirit is the proactive path that God calls every man to follow.

A second passage that is critical to our biblical strategy for victory is Colossians 3:5: "Put to death, therefore, whatever belongs to your earthly nature: sexual immorality, impurity, lust, evil desires and greed, which is idolatry." We are to put to death the sins of passion in our lives. These sins have the potential to consume us, capture us, and become the idols we worship. The Goliath of lust must be put to death in order for us to experience victory.

Every martial arts fan has heard of Bruce Lee. He is an icon in the world of martial arts movies and in the history of the sport. One of the reasons Bruce Lee is so popular is because of the mystery surrounding his death. As a young man, in the prime of his acting career, Bruce Lee died mysteriously in Hong Kong. The autopsy was inconclusive as to the cause and so the rumors abound. Some believe that Bruce Lee died of *Dim Mak. Dim Mak*, or "touch of death," is a secret blow that results in the death of an opponent. When this touch of death is rendered properly, the recipient's organs, at the point of the strike, begin to shut down and die. Someone who has received a *Dim Mak* punch dies mysteriously within a few days of the punch. Many believe that a practitioner applied a *Dim Mak* punch to Bruce Lee, and as a result, he died an untimely death.

Every godly man needs to deliver a Dim Mak *punch to lust.* We must put to death sexual immorality, lust and sinful passions. This requires a serious and calculated decision. We must decide that we are going to follow Jesus Christ no matter what it takes; we are going to pursue godliness, and we are not going to tolerate idols in our lives. Putting to death the idol of lust is a necessary step for any man who truly desires to defeat this Goliath.

A third passage that helps us develop a strategy for facing the Goliath of lust is 1 Corinthians 6:18-20:

> Flee from sexual immorality. All other sins a man commits are outside his body, but he who sins sexually sins against his own body. Do you not know that your body is a temple of the Holy Spirit, who is in you, whom you have received from God? You are not your own; you were bought at a price. Therefore honor God with your body.

We are to honor God with our bodies. Sexual sin becomes enslaving and captures even our bodies. Since, as new men in Christ, we have the Holy Spirit indwelling us, we are to flee sexual immorality and honor God with our bodies. This passage is a strong warning and command to "run away from sin." Our sense of sin's destructiveness, as well as our desire to please Christ, should lead us to radically do whatever we have to do to flee the temptation of sexual immorality.

We are to be like Joseph in the Old Testament. Joseph was sold into slavery but quickly distinguished himself in the house of Potiphar, his master. Joseph was put in charge of all of the household duties and entrusted with everything Potiphar owned. But Joseph was a good-looking young man, and Potiphar's wife had the hots for him. Day after day, Potiphar's wife would come to Joseph and in essence sing Marvin Gay's "Let's Get it On." One day she cornered him, grabbed him, and tried to seduce him. What did Joseph do? He made like a bakery truck and hauled buns! Joseph applied 1 Corinthians 6:18—he literally fled sexual immorality (see Gen. 39:1-12). When the Goliath of lust stands in our path, we are to resist temptation. *Sometimes the best way to resist is to run in the opposite direction!*

A final Scripture that helps us put together a game plan to defeat Goliath is Matthew 4:1-11:

> Then Jesus was led by the Spirit into the desert to be tempted by the devil. After fasting forty days and forty nights, he was hungry. The tempter came to him and said, "If you are the Son of God, tell these stones to become bread."
>
> Jesus answered, "It is written: 'Man does not live on bread alone, but on every word that comes from the mouth of God.'"
>
> Then the devil took him to the holy city and had him stand on the highest point of the temple. "If you are the Son of God," he said, "throw yourself down. For it is written: 'He will command his angels concerning you, and they will lift you up in their hands, so that you will not strike your foot against a stone.'"
>
> Jesus answered him, "It is also written: 'Do not put the Lord your God to the test.'"
>
> Again, the devil took him to a very high mountain and showed him all the kingdoms of the world and their splendor. "All this I will give you," he said, "if you will bow down and worship me."
>
> Jesus said to him, "Away from me, Satan! For it is written: 'Worship the Lord your God, and serve him only.'"
>
> Then the devil left him, and angels came and attended him.

Satan came to Jesus and tempted Him three times. Each temptation was an appeal to the human desires of Jesus. As the eternal Son of God, Jesus could have just squashed the devil like a bug. But as the perfect man, Jesus surrendered to the Holy Spirit and depended completely on the Word of God. He responded to each temptation by trusting in the authority of Scripture and quoting God's Word back to the devil. Jesus was victorious because He used the sword of the Spirit, which is the Word of God.

When we use God's Word as a weapon to deflect and defeat temptation, we experience the victory of Jesus Christ. The authority and truthfulness of the Word of God overcomes the Goliath of lust. The enemy's tool is deception, but God's weapon is the truth that sets us free. We are to bring every thought, every temptation and every fantasy into the light of Scripture; when we do, the devil is stopped in his tracks. Peter urges us, "Therefore, prepare your minds for action; be self-controlled; set your hope fully on the grace to be given you when Jesus Christ is revealed" (1 Pet. 1:13). When our minds are prepared for action, we recognize the Goliath of lust, and we are ready to respond with the Word of God.

From the Scriptures used in this chapter, here is a starter pack of verses you can use to speak back to the devil when he seeks to attack you through the Goliath of lust:

> Flee from sexual immorality. All other sins a man commits are outside his body, but he who sins sexually sins against his own body. Do you not know that your body is a temple of the Holy Spirit, who is in you, whom you have received from God? You are not your own; you were bought at a price. Therefore honor God with your body (1 Cor. 6:18-20).

> Put to death, therefore, whatever belongs to your earthly nature: sexual immorality, impurity, lust, evil desires and greed, which is idolatry (Col. 3:5).

> But I say, walk by the Spirit, and you will not carry out the desire of the flesh (Gal. 5:16, *NASB*).

No temptation has seized you except what is common to man. And God is faithful; he will not let you be tempted beyond what you can bear. But when you are tempted, he will also provide a way out so that you can stand up under it (1 Cor. 10:13).

Therefore, prepare your minds for action; be self-controlled; set your hope fully on the grace to be given you when Jesus Christ is revealed (1 Pet. 1:13).

Every man faces Goliaths in life; for many of us, one of those Goliaths is lust. We can have confidence of spiritual victory when we protect ourselves from being vulnerable and when we execute a biblical game plan for winning the battle. Remember, the battle belongs to the Lord.

Discussion

See It
Read 1 Samuel 17:1-11,16,24.

- What is the natural human response when a man faces a Goliath?

- For most men, lust is a constant Goliath. How does lust defeat a man and become an obstacle to his seeking after Christ?

Discuss It
- Read 2 Samuel 11:1-5. How did David become entangled by the Goliath of lust?

- Based on David's example, what makes a man vulnerable to being defeated by his own lusts?

- Look up the following verses and discuss the Bible's warnings and instructions about dealing with lust: 1 John 2:15-17; James 1:13-15; Romans 13:14; Galatians 5:17; Colossians 3:5; Romans 8:12-13.

Do It

- Based on the above Scriptures, what commitment does God want you to make when facing the Goliath of lust?

- What is God's promise in 1 Corinthians 10:13? What does this promise mean to you?

- What action steps can you take to claim God's promise and be victorious over lust?

7

FACING THE GOLIATH OF ANGER

Like David—and like every other man—you will at some point walk into the Valley of Elah and come face to face with the enemy. Your Goliath may be anger. This Goliath hurls taunts and leaves broken and scarred victims in its path. You may struggle with uncontrolled rage or maybe just passive-aggressive responses—but either way, your heart is constantly in turmoil rather than being ruled by the peace of Christ. This was the struggle of King Saul:

> When the men were returning home after David had killed the Philistine, the women came out from all the towns of Israel to meet King Saul with singing and dancing, with joyful songs and with tambourines and lutes. As they danced, they sang: "Saul has slain his thousands, and David his tens of thousands." Saul was very angry; this refrain galled him. "They have credited David with tens of thousands," he thought, "but me with only thousands. What more can he get but the kingdom?" And from that time on Saul kept a jealous eye on David (1 Sam. 18:6-9).

Anger can have many causes: unfulfilled expectations, blocked goals, traumatic circumstances, difficult people, biochemical change, and even direct demonic attack. For Saul, his anger was fueled by jealousy. Saul was jealous of the attention that David received. David was the competition to Saul's praise and adulation. David was the new kid on the block, and everyone was enamored with him. Saul was selfish; he wanted to be number one in people's eyes, and he became jealous and angry at David's success.

Saul's jealousy caused him to have an angry attitude toward David. Underneath the surface of his kingly response, Saul harbored anger in his heart. This anger eventually found an unrighteous outlet. First Samuel 18:10-11 tells the story:

> The next day an evil spirit from God came forcefully upon Saul. He was prophesying in his house, while David was playing the harp, as he usually did. Saul had a spear in his hand and he hurled it, saying to himself, "I'll pin David to the wall." But David eluded him twice.

Saul's anger, left unchecked, unconfessed and without repentance, expressed itself in violent action. Saul tried to kill David. The text says, "The next day an evil spirit from God came forcefully upon Saul." A demonic spirit, allowed access by God, took advantage of Saul's sinful anger and deceived him into acting with murderous intent. Sinful anger is a Goliath that can have terrible consequences.

I mentioned a moment ago that anger can have multiple origins. Suppose I am driving on the freeway, minding my own business, when all of a sudden a speeding driver zooms past me and unsafely changes lanes, cutting me off. In response, I hit the horn, and then that jerk . . . oh, sorry, I was venting my own experience from this morning's commute! Seriously, it could be as simple as being cut off on the freeway. Or maybe my wife says something to me in a disrespectful tone and I think, *I deserve better than that.* Rather than letting it go, I stew on it all day—and by the time I get home, and my wife warmly greets me at the door, I am mad and either vent my frustration or do the passive-aggressive thing and give her the silent treatment. Sometimes anger is a systemic thing that is rooted in unresolved conflict or painful experiences from the past.

Many years ago, when I was in my first pastorate, I went through a season of anger. People bugged me. I felt like everyone had expectations of me, and I could either establish personal boundaries and disappoint them, or I could try to live by what other people wanted and lose myself. I felt screwed either way. (Pardon my French, but that was how I felt.) This was my first job as a senior pastor, and I truly wanted to serve and be a success, so I went for option B—and I became increasingly frustrated. It reached a point where I knew that I needed outside help and counsel. A friend of mine was a Christian counselor, so I invited him to lunch to discuss the problem.

As I unpacked the issues, he said he was aware of the church's culture and that I was dealing with some unhealthy people.

"Yeah," I said, "but I'm not handling it well and I need some help."

So, I scheduled an appointment to meet with him at his office. We began to talk, and he asked me a lot of questions about my life, my history and my family. I told him that my father had died when I was young, and that my mom had kept the family together—that she was an awesome lady. He asked me to share an early memory of my father. I flashed back to an argument I remember my parents having when I was only eight years old.

My dad had lung cancer, and in those days the treatments were very limited. One of his lungs had been removed, and he had undergone radiation treatment on his remaining lung. We had always been poor, but with my dad sick and unable to work, we had no income for our family. My mom didn't know how to drive and didn't have a job; we literally depended upon neighbors who would leave bags of groceries on our porch. Now as a kid, I wasn't aware of all the issues, just the tension they created.

On this particular day, I had come home from school and found my parents having an argument. My mom was concerned about our family and our finances; my dad, typical of men of his generation, didn't discuss these kinds of things with my mom. As I recounted this story in the counselor's office, I shared what I remembered of the dialogue.

My dad screamed, "I'm going to take care of this family; don't worry."

My mom answered, "But you're sick and you can't work. What are we going to do?"

My dad yelled back, "I'll get a job."

I'd been standing there, watching my parents. Now I looked up at my dad and said, "Daddy, when are you going to look for a job? You're always lying down in your chair."

At that, my dad, who was a big man at 6' 4", rose up and screamed at me, "I'll get a job! I'll get a job!"

"J. P., do you hear yourself? J. P. . . . ." It was my friend the therapist talking to me.

I had become so engrossed in telling the story, I had become lost in the memory. "What?" I said.

"Do you hear yourself? Do you hear how you are talking?"

All of a sudden, I became aware of the way I was telling the story. My voice was like an imitation of a little boy.

My friend said, "You are talking like you are still that little eight-year-old kid."

When he said that, out of nowhere, with the force of uncontrolled emotion, I began to weep—and then to really weep! I felt like a flood gate had opened, and I couldn't stop crying. I felt free but I also felt embarrassed. As I cried, I thought, *Uh-oh, now he is going to think I am really nuts!*

The counselor asked me some more questions, and he seemed to be looking right into my soul. As my appointment came to a close, he smiled at me and said, "J. P., I don't think you have an anger problem. You have a shame problem. You internalized very early that you should be the helper, the good child, the perfect child. Somewhere along the way, you came to believe that when people around you were not happy, somehow that was your fault. You have carried a burden that you were never meant to have. Your anger is the warning sign that people are pushing your shame button. When people put expectations on you, and you feel the burden to meet them, you get overloaded. You begin to resent the very people you love and want to serve, because you fear that you can't give them what they need. You wrongly feel that you are supposed to be the one who can meet their needs. Your anger is really the result of the shame you are feeling. It's not just that you did something bad; you are feeling like you are bad. You are feeling like that eight-year-old boy who made his dad mad—when really your dad was taking his anger and his shame out on you. Your healing process is about dealing with shame, the cause of your anger."

Those words of truth both cut and brought healing to my soul. The presenting issue was anger, but the cause was shame. Like Saul—and like me—every man faces the Goliath of anger—and that anger is caused by something. Part of the healing process, and a step on the path to victory, is discovering the source of our anger. David once prayed this prayer:

> Search me, O God, and know my heart; test me and know my anxious thoughts. See if there is any offensive way in me, and lead me in the way everlasting (Ps. 139:23-24).

Maybe you need to pray the prayer of David. Ask God to show you why anger churns in your soul. Ask Him why you feel frustrated and out of control. *Ask Him to search your heart and to reveal to you the cause of your anger—and then, surrender your entire heart to Jesus.* Ask Him to lead you in the everlasting way. You may need a trusted friend or pastor or counselor to help you identify the cause of your anger. Whatever the cause, Jesus Christ can bring healing, forgiveness and transformation.

We face the Goliath of anger when we open up our hearts to Jesus Christ. We ask Jesus for His grace and His truth to heal us and set us free. We need a gospel-centered game plan to defeat this Goliath. God gives us just that in Ephesians 4:

> Surely you heard of him and were taught in him in accordance with the truth that is in Jesus. You were taught, with regard to your former way of life, to put off your old self, which is being corrupted by its deceitful desires; to be made new in the attitude of your minds; and to put on the new self, created to be like God in true righteousness and holiness (vv. 21-24).

Paul argues that our salvation was a complete conversion. We put off our old self and put on our new self. We are now being renewed in the attitude of our minds. God is making us like Himself in true righteousness and holiness. Paul uses the terms "put off" and "put on." These words are also used to describe taking off dirty clothes and putting on clean clothes.

Playing football my senior year in high school, like many athletes, I was superstitious. My good-luck charm was my shirt that I wore under my shoulder pads and jersey. After practice, my shirt would be soaking wet from sweat. I would hang it up in my locker, and the next day, after it had been dried out by the night's air, I would put that dirty stiff shirt back on. I managed to wear the same undershirt all season without washing it one time! Gross, I know, but like the commercial says, "It's only weird if it doesn't work."

From a rational perspective, the idea of putting on a dirty, sweaty shirt is incongruous. In the same way, when we, who are new men in Christ, put back on the "clothes of our old nature," it doesn't make sense. We are new men; we put off the old man. What makes sense is to put on the clean clothes of love, mercy, kindness, justice, compassion, humility and all the fruit of the Spirit. We have been converted; we live the Christian life as new men in Christ who are in a process of being renewed.

This is the foundation for Paul's words that follow. He is about to give us a game plan for defeating the Goliath of anger, but first he reminds us that we live out of our identity in Christ. *As men who have put off the old nature and have put on our new identity in Christ, we have the resources to fight the Goliath of anger.* Paul gives us these instructions:

> Therefore each of you must put off falsehood and speak truthfully to his neighbor, for we are all members of one body. "In your anger do not sin": Do not let the sun go down while you are still angry, and do not give the devil a foothold. He who has been stealing must steal no longer, but must work, doing something useful with his own hands, that he may have something to share with those in need.

Do not let any unwholesome talk come out of your mouths, but only what is helpful for building others up according to their needs, that it may benefit those who listen. And do not grieve the Holy Spirit of God, with whom you were sealed for the day of redemption. Get rid of all bitterness, rage and anger, brawling and slander, along with every form of malice. Be kind and compassionate to one another, forgiving each other, just as in Christ God forgave you (Eph. 4:25-32).

Paul's game plan to fight the Goliath of anger includes several proactive steps. These are positive and negative commands that we need to obey. Every man needs:

1. To put off falsehood and speak truthfully
2. To be angry but not to sin
3. To not let the sun go down while he is angry
4. To not give the devil a foothold
5. To stop stealing, and to work in order to have something to share with those in need
6. To not let unwholesome talk come out of his mouth, but to speak what builds others up
7. To not grieve the Holy Spirit
8. To get rid of all bitterness, rage and anger, brawling and slander, and malice
9. To be kind, compassionate and forgiving

Each of these actions requires a decision, a commitment and initiative. We will never defeat the Goliath of anger with a passive, wimpy approach to change. It takes the "I do" part of our character. As a pastor, I have had the privilege of presiding over many marriage ceremonies. The people getting married love each other and are committed to becoming husband and wife. Within the ceremony, there is a section known as the "pledge of commitment." I ask both man and woman if they will love their spouse, be faithful to them, honor them and serve them. At the end of the pledge, I instruct both bride and groom, "If so, say, 'I do.'" It is in saying "I do" that a person truly commits himself to action. We need to say "I do" to the actions described in Ephesians 4:25-32 if we are going to take the fight to the enemy and defeat the Goliath of anger.

The first commitment we must make is to lay aside falsehood and speak truthfully. Lies and deceit are a natural breeding ground for anger to grow. It is the truth that sets us free; when we have relationships based on truth, anger is squashed before it has a chance to permeate our lives.

But not all anger is sin. Anger can be a positive and righteous response. God gets angry. The trick is to get angry at the right things and be angry in the right way. This is why we are commanded to be angry but not to sin. When we are righteously angry, we are under the control of the Holy Spirit and manifest the fruit of the Spirit. Anger, however, is volatile, and we can easily move from righteous anger to sinful anger. So, we are warned and commanded not to let the sun go down while we are angry.

In other words, deal with anger quickly. Don't put it on the back burner, where it will continue to simmer and affect your attitude, actions and relationships. The Goliath of destructive anger is most likely to explode when it has been on a slow burn for a long time in our lives. Deal with it. Talk about it; speak truthfully and let the truth set you free. These verses exhort us to be honest about our anger and to deal with it in the realm of truth. When we do, we keep our anger in check, we experience it righteously, and we do not give the devil a foothold in our lives.

Another step in our game plan to defeat the Goliath of anger in our lives is to move from a self-centered attitude to an others-centered attitude. We are to stop stealing and work so that we can share with those who are in need. If we steal, we are acting with disregard toward others and with a selfish regard for ourselves. Selfishness fuels anger because it is a deceived perspective. We think it's all about us.

When I am pressured for time, running late and rushing to an appointment, it seems that everyone on the road is a slow-poke cautious driver. I become frustrated—I talk to myself, have arguments with myself, and lose arguments with myself! In reality, people aren't driving any differently than they normally do. What is different is that I am focused on myself; I am being selfish. With a selfish attitude, I am vulnerable to the Goliath of anger.

So, what do we do to combat the attitude of selfishness? God's answer in Ephesians 4:28 is that we work hard so that we can serve those in need. We take our eyes off ourselves and ask, "How can I give back and serve the people in need around me?" When our emotional energy is flowing outward in service, it is not being used up inwardly in selfish anger.

The next element in the game plan to defeat the Goliath of anger is the use of our words. Words can build up or they can destroy. Angry words hurt; encouraging, grace-filled words bless. Paul says, "Do not let any unwholesome talk come out of your mouths, but only what is helpful for building others up according to their needs, that it may benefit those who listen" (v. 29). Unwholesome words are words that tear down, attack, shame, criticize, belittle and accuse. These are personal attacks designed to tear down and hurt others. Jesus said that these kinds of words come out of the heart (see Mark 7:21-22). If our hearts are dominated by the Goliath of anger, then our words will be cutting and destructive. The man who has put off the old nature, and has put on a new identity in Christ, has received a new heart. We are to ask Jesus to fill and renew our hearts so that what comes out of them is not cursing but blessing.

Our words have the power to bless or to curse. Peter exhorts, "Finally, all of you, live in harmony with one another; be sympathetic, love as brothers, be compassionate and humble. Do not repay evil with evil or insult with insult, but with blessing, because to this you were called so that you may inherit a blessing" (1 Pet. 3:8-9). God's call on our lives is that we are to be a blessing. Our words can bless with grace, or they can curse with unwholesome talk.

Do you want to add grace to someone's life? Bless them with words that impart grace. Do you recognize that your words are not filled with grace? Then realize that you need to internalize grace. The more grace you get into your life, the more your words will spread grace.

When we speak unwholesome words, we actually steal grace from people, and we grieve the Holy Spirit. The proactive action we need to take in fighting the Goliath of anger is to stop all unwholesome conversation and instead speak words of grace that build others up.

Paul concludes his call to action by reminding us of our original conversion experience. Back in verses 22-24, he described our salvation as putting off the old nature and putting on the new nature in Christ. Now he picks that analogy back up, saying:

> Get rid of all bitterness, rage and anger, brawling and slander, along with every form of malice. Be kind and compassionate to one another, forgiving each other, just as in Christ God forgave you (vv. 31-32).

As if we were taking off dirty clothes, we should get rid of bitterness, rage, brawling, slander and malice. These actions are not part of our new identity in Christ; they are the result of being dominated by the Goliath of anger. We need to see them for what they are: destructive, sinful and the antithesis of Christlike behavior. Then we need to get rid of them. As new men in Christ, we need to cultivate, develop and put on kindness, compassion and forgiveness. When we demonstrate these qualities, we are truly following Jesus.

The commands of Ephesians 4:25-32 can only be embraced and followed when we have been truly converted to Christ. *The man who has put off his old nature and put on his new identity in Christ is the man who can draw upon the resources of Christ in his life to fight Goliath.* The Goliath of anger taunts, deceives and tempts every man, but the new man in Christ can recognize this Goliath and face him in Christ's name. We can turn our anger over to Christ. We can ask Christ for His forgiveness. We can internalize Christ's grace, and we can express Christ's compassion. This is the game plan for facing the Goliath of anger.

Discussion

See It

Read 1 Samuel 17:10-11,16,24.

- What happens to a man if his eyes are not on God's resources for victory when he faces Goliath?

- How can Goliaths become patterns of behavior, sinful habits or enslaving addictions?

Discuss It

- A common Goliath that men face is anger. How can the human emotion of anger become dysfunctional and destructive in a man's life?

- Read 1 Samuel 18:10-29. How did anger become a Goliath in Saul's life?

- What were the negative effects of Saul's anger on himself, his relationship with others, and his relationship with God?

- What do the following verses say about dysfunctional and destructive anger: James 1:19-20; Proverbs 20:2; Proverbs 27:4; Proverbs 29:22; Proverbs 30:33?

Do It

- The only way to deal with anger is through a gospel-centered strategy. Read the following verses and discover what they say about how a man can experience God's game plan for victory over anger: Ephesians 5:18-21; Ephesians 4:25-32; James 1:18-22.

- What is your next step in applying God's resources to deal with the Goliath of anger?

8

FACING GOLIATH
WITH THE TRUTH OF
THE GOSPEL

Every man is on a spiritual journey. The most important step in the journey is to cross the line into a personal relationship with Jesus Christ. That happens when we believe the gospel, which is the good news of God's salvation. More precisely, the gospel is the good news about the bad news!

"What's the bad news?" you ask. The Bible is clear that every man has a sin problem: "For all have sinned and fall short of the glory of God" (Rom. 3:23). Sin is falling short of God's glory; it is failing to be who God created us to be and failing to do what God has commanded us to do. Every person is measured by the perfect love and holiness of God—and falls short. Every person willfully chooses to do their own thing rather than obey God's commands, and is therefore guilty of disobeying God. The bad news is that we are sinners, and the penalty for sin is death: "For the wages of sin is death, but the gift of God is eternal life in Christ Jesus our Lord" (Rom. 6:23). The Bible reveals that death, in all its forms, is a result of sin. Physical death, spiritual death and eternal death are all results of sin. Every man is a sinner—and left to his own devices, every man will suffer the full consequences of his sin. This is the bad news of the gospel.

Some time ago, I was sitting next to a man on a plane. We exchanged greetings, and soon we were engaged in a deep spiritual conversation. As I explained the good news and the bad news of the gospel, he took exception to the idea that he was a sinner. I took out a yellow legal pad and drew a graph on the page. At the top of the page I wrote the word "God," and in parentheses I wrote "perfect." I drew a line down the page; at the bottom, I wrote the word "man," and in parentheses I wrote "the worst sinner." I explained what I had written, and then I handed the man my pen.

"On the graph, plot where you think you are in terms of your moral standing and responsibility to God," I instructed him. Looking at the graph, he began to make a mark; before he did, I asked him, "Have you ever heard of Billy Graham?" He replied that he had, so I said, "Billy Graham would place himself at the bottom of the graph."

"Hmm," he replied.

Again he began to make a mark on the graph, and again I interrupted him: "Have you ever heard of Mother Teresa?"

"Of course," he answered.

"Well, Mother Teresa would place herself at the bottom, as well."

Now he got a perplexed and frustrated look on his face. "Well, I know I am not better than Billy Graham or Mother Teresa!" he blurted out.

I went on to explain that all of us are sinful and separated from God, and that none of us can bridge that separation through our own efforts. That's the bad news of the gospel.

The good news of the gospel is that Jesus Christ lived a perfect life, died on the cross to pay the penalty for our sin, and rose victorious over sin and death. The apostle Paul asserts, "For what I received I passed on to you as of first importance: that Christ died for our sins according to the Scriptures, that he was buried, that he was raised on the third day according to the Scriptures" (1 Cor. 15:3-4). Christ is the bridge that connects us to God. He is the only way to have our sins forgiven and to be reconciled to a holy God. Jesus Himself said, "I am the way and the truth and the life. No one comes to the Father except through Me" (John 14:6). The reason Jesus is the only way to God is that He is the unique God-Man—and He is the only substitute that takes away our sin. His unique death is accepted by God as a payment for our sin, and His resurrection gives authority to His claim that He is able to forgive our sin and give us eternal life.

We receive this truth of the gospel by faith. As Paul says, "It is by grace you have been saved, through faith—and this not from yourselves, it is the gift of God—not by works, so that no one can boast" (Eph. 2:8-9). God saves us by grace alone, through faith alone in Christ alone. Salvation is the good news about the bad news. God saves us from the penalty and power of sin. He defeats Goliath and gives us His victory! This salvation victory is available to any man who calls on the name of the Lord:

> If you confess with your mouth, "Jesus is Lord," and be-lieve in your heart that God raised him from the dead, you will be saved. For it is with your heart that you believe and are justified, and it is with your mouth that you confess and are saved. As the Scripture says, "Anyone who trusts in him will never be put to shame." For there is no difference between Jew and Gentile—the same Lord is Lord of all and richly blesses all who call on him, for, "Everyone who calls on the name of the Lord will be saved" (Rom. 10:9-13).

At my church, we refer to the act of calling on the Lord for sal-vation as "crossing the line."

Several years ago, at a men's retreat, I addressed a large audi-ence of men sitting in an outdoor amphitheater. Behind the stage where I was speaking was a rustic wooden cross. In my message, I explained the bad news and the good news of salvation in Christ. I then took a long rope, stretched it across the front of the gather-ing, and challenged the men to call on Christ for salvation—to sur-render their whole lives to Him, and to get up from where they were seated and symbolically "cross the line." From all over the amphitheater, men arose from their seats and crossed the line into salvation. Since that first retreat, I have used this metaphor many times to explain to men God's offer of salvation in Christ and their need to repent and receive Christ by faith.

What about you? Have you crossed the line? Have you called on God to save you from your sin through His provision in Jesus Christ? If you have never made that decision, or if you do not have the assurance that your sins are forgiven and that Christ is in your life, would you like to receive Him right now? If so, please make my prayer your own. There is nothing magic about these words, but they express a repentant heart and an attitude of faith. Use the following prayer to call on the Lord and ask Him to save you—to give you the confidence that Christ alone is your Savior and that He will never let you go:

> *Lord Jesus, I admit that I am a sinner and that I cannot save myself. I believe that You died on the cross for my sins, and that You rose from the dead. Jesus, forgive my sins and come into my life. I repent and receive You as my Savior and Lord. Take control of my life and be my Lord for the rest of my life. I surrender to You, and I thank You that You will never leave me nor forsake me. In Jesus' name. Amen!*

If you sincerely prayed that prayer and asked Jesus into your life, then on the authority of God's Word, you can know that God heard your cry and has given you eternal life. This promise is for you:

> Anyone who believes in the Son of God has this testimony in his heart. Anyone who does not believe God has made him out to be a liar, because he has not believed the testimony God has given about his Son. And this is the testimony: God has given us eternal life, and this life is in his Son. He who has the Son has life; he who does not have the Son of God does not have life. I write these things to you who believe in the name of the Son of God so that you may know that you have eternal life (1 John 5:10-13).

God has given us eternal life. That life is found in God's Son, Jesus Christ. If you have the Son, then you have the life; but if you do not have the Son, then you do not have eternal life. If you believe in the name of God's Son, then you can know with certainty that you have eternal life. God wants every one of His men to have the confidence that Christ is in their life and that they have eternal life.

Now, about this time, some of you are thinking, *This sounds great, but what does it have to do with facing my Goliath?* It has everything to do with facing Goliath! We face and defeat the Goliaths in our lives with the truth of the gospel. You see, the story of David and Goliath illustrates the bad news and the good news of the gospel. First, there is an enemy that is insurmountable in our own strength. This enemy taunts us, intimidates us, and—unless it is defeated—enslaves us. This is sin; this is the devil; this is Goliath. This is the bad news. However, God provides a way of salvation. The battle is the Lord's. He is our Savior. David, looking at the enemy, rejects the armor of Saul. He says, "I can't fight in these." This is David's declaration that he cannot save himself; his only hope is to trust in the Lord. David, trusting in God, walks into the Valley of Elah and experiences God's victory over Goliath. David shows us that every man must turn from his resources and trust in Christ alone to forgive his sins and give him the victory. We face Goliath with the truth of gospel.

The gospel declares that we are new men in Jesus Christ: "Therefore, if anyone is in Christ, he is a new creation; the old has gone, the new has come!" (2 Cor. 5:17). When we call on the Lord, cross the line and believe in Jesus Christ, God makes us new people and gives us a new spiritual identity. The truest thing about us is what God says is true! When we know what is true about us because of the gospel, and when we live in our new gospel identity, we can have spiritual authority to resist and defeat our Goliaths. Jesus said, "You will know the truth, and the truth will set you free" (John 8:32).

The good news of the gospel can be understood in terms of three categories: the work of Christ, the gift of the Holy Spirit, and our identification with Christ. Each of these doctrines unfolds for us what God has made true for every believer in Christ. The truest thing about us is what God says is true. Because of the work of Jesus Christ, as God's men, we have justification, redemption, propitiation and reconciliation. These are not just theological words; these terms describe our gospel blessings and resources to fight the spiritual battle. As Paul asserts:

> But now a righteousness from God, apart from law, has been made known, to which the Law and the Prophets testify. This righteousness from God comes through faith in Jesus Christ to all who believe. There is no difference, for all have sinned and fall short of the glory of God, and are *justified* freely by his grace through the *redemption* that came by Christ Jesus. God presented him as a *sacrifice of atonement*, through faith in his blood. He did this to demonstrate his justice, because in his forbearance he had left the sins committed beforehand unpunished—he did it to demonstrate his justice at the present time, so as to be just and *the one who justifies* those who have faith in Jesus.
> Where, then, is boasting? It is excluded. On what principle? On that of observing the law? No, but on that of faith. For we maintain that a man is *justified* by faith apart from observing the law. Is God the God of Jews only? Is he not the God of Gentiles too? Yes, of Gentiles too, since there is only one God, who will *justify* the circumcised by faith and the uncircumcised through that same faith (Rom. 3:21-30, emphasis added).

Paul explains the gospel by answering a question. The question is: How can a holy and just God have fellowship with sinful man? Paul's answer is that God must remove the barrier of sin and pronounce us righteous through faith in Jesus Christ. God is righteous, so the only way we can have a relationship with Him is for us to be righteous as well. Since we are dead in sin, none of us can become righteous in and of ourselves. We must receive an alien righteousness. God declares us righteous and gives us His righteousness when we place our faith in Jesus Christ. This is the truth of justification. Justification is God's judgment declaring us not guilty, and beyond that, positively righteous in Jesus Christ.

The metaphor is a courtroom where we are the accused and God is the judge. The truth is that we are guilty. But Jesus Christ died as a righteous substitute for our sin. When we put our faith in Jesus Christ, God, the righteous judge, pronounces us not guilty. He declares us righteous and imparts to us His righteousness. This is true because God says it is true.

When Goliath accuses you, tempts you and seeks to take you down, you can stand on the truth of your righteousness in Jesus Christ. Remember, the truest thing about you is what God says is true!

Because of the work of Jesus Christ, you not only have justification, but you also have redemption. The metaphor behind the idea of redemption is the purchase of a slave from the slave market. In the ancient world, slaves were bought and sold based upon an agreement on the purchase price. Once the price was paid, the slave could be set free by the purchaser. Every man is born into slavery to sin. Our only hope is for the purchase price to be paid. When Jesus Christ died on the cross, He shed His blood and purchased our freedom from sin's slavery.

If you were to go to Home Depot—which every man knows is the adult version of Toys 'R' Us—you would find all kinds of tools and home improvement items. Every item has a sticker with a bar code on it. The bar code records the price of that item, and when the bar code is scanned, the price appears on the register screen. If you want to legally take an item from Home Depot, you must pay the purchase price. When you pay the price, the item becomes yours.

Jesus paid the price for our sins, so we belong to Him. His blood set us free from bondage to sin, and now we have a new master—Jesus Christ.

When Goliath stands in the path blocking your progress, or shouts his lies that you must obey his lusts, you can tell him that you have a new master. You are not a slave to sin. You are forgiven and covered by the blood of Jesus Christ. You have been set free and do not have to obey his temptations or surrender to his threats. You have justification and redemption in Jesus Christ. The truest thing about you is what God says is true!

The passage from Romans quoted above describes how we are justified and redeemed in Jesus Christ. It also explains how the work of Christ has secured propitiation for us. The *New International Version* of the Bible uses the phrase "sacrifice of atonement." The Greek word is *hilasterion,* which means a covering. In particular, the term refers to the covering of atonement provided by the sacrificial blood sprinkled in the holy of holies over the Ark of the Covenant. (Remember *Raiders of the Lost Ark*? That's the Ark we're talking about.)

The Ark was placed in the holy of holies, and upon it sat the Mercy Seat. This is where once a year, on the Day of Atonement, the high priest would sprinkle the blood (see Lev. 16). God, because of His justice, demanded a punishment for sin. But because God was merciful as well as just, He accepted the blood of a substitute and did not punish the people for their sins. This is propitiation. God accepts the sacrifice of Jesus Christ as a substitute punishment for our sins. His justice and wrath toward sin are satisfied, and His mercy is expressed toward those who come to Him through the work of Christ.

When Goliath accuses you and seeks to defeat you through guilt and shame, you can say, "I am forgiven in Jesus Christ. I have been set free. I am not condemned. God loves me and fully accepts me." The truest thing about you is what God says is true. God says that Jesus Christ has made propitiation for your sins. God's justice and mercy are vindicated. God is not mad at you, and you will never suffer the wrath of God for your sins. Propitiation assures you that a holy God accepts you and loves you in Jesus Christ.

The work of Jesus Christ gives us justification, redemption and propitiation. The work of Christ also gives us reconciliation. Let's look at another passage from Paul's letter to the Romans:

> But God demonstrates his own love for us in this: While we were still sinners, Christ died for us. Since we have now been justified by his blood, how much more shall we be saved from God's wrath through him! For if, when we were God's enemies, we were *reconciled* to him through the death of his Son, how much more, having been *reconciled,*

shall we be saved through his life! Not only is this so, but we also rejoice in God through our Lord Jesus Christ, through whom we have now received *reconciliation* (Rom. 5:8-11, emphasis added).

We have been reconciled to God through Jesus Christ. The backdrop to the idea of reconciliation is a broken relationship. Reconciliation is the removal of the barrier that alienates two parties, so that enemies can become friends. Because of the barrier of sin, men are enemies of God. Picture God being on one side of the Grand Canyon and humanity on the other side; the chasm is so great that no human action can bridge the distance. The good news of the gospel is that Jesus Christ is the bridge that connects us to God. Christ has removed the barrier of sin so that we, who by nature and choice have been God's enemies, can become His friends.

Whatever your Goliath may be, its intent is to alienate you from God. The truth of reconciliation is that you are no longer God's enemy. Even when you were a sinner, Christ died for you and demonstrated His love for you. You are a friend of God and you have an eternal relationship with God. The lie of the enemy is that God has turned His back on you, or that you have turned your back on God in a way that has alienated you from Him once more. The truth is that because of the work of Christ, you have been permanently reconciled to God. The truest thing about you is what God says is true!

The truths of our salvation are brought about by the work of Christ and by the gift of the Holy Spirit. The Holy Spirit is the third person of the Trinity. He is co-equal with the Father and the Son. When we receive salvation, God sends the Holy Spirit into our lives, and He gives us a new nature. *At salvation, through the work of the Holy Spirit, every believer has been born again, indwelt, sealed, baptized and adopted into God's family by the Spirit.* Consider the following Scriptures that describe the gift of the Holy Spirit:

But when the kindness and love of God our Savior appeared, he saved us, not because of righteous things we had done, but because of his mercy. He saved us through the washing of rebirth and renewal by the Holy Spirit, whom he poured out on us generously through Jesus Christ our Savior (Titus 3:4-6).

In reply Jesus declared, "I tell you the truth, no one can see the kingdom of God unless he is born again."

"How can a man be born when he is old?" Nicodemus asked. "Surely he cannot enter a second time into his mother's womb to be born!"

Jesus answered, "I tell you the truth, no one can enter the kingdom of God unless he is born of water and the Spirit. Flesh gives birth to flesh, but the Spirit gives birth to spirit. You should not be surprised at my saying, 'You must be born again.' The wind blows wherever it pleases. You hear its sound, but you cannot tell where it comes from or where it is going. So it is with everyone born of the Spirit" (John 3:3-8).

You, however, are controlled not by the sinful nature but by the Spirit, if the Spirit of God lives in you. And if anyone does not have the Spirit of Christ, he does not belong to Christ. But if Christ is in you, your body is dead because of sin, yet your spirit is alive because of righteousness. And if the Spirit of him who raised Jesus from the dead is living in you, he who raised Christ from the dead will also give life to your mortal bodies through his Spirit, who lives in you (Rom. 8:9-11).

And you also were included in Christ when you heard the word of truth, the gospel of your salvation. Having believed, you were marked in him with a seal, the promised Holy Spirit, who is a deposit guaranteeing our inheritance until the redemption of those who are God's possession— to the praise of his glory (Eph. 1:13-14).

For we were all baptized by one Spirit into one body—whether Jews or Greeks, slave or free—and we were all given the one Spirit to drink (1 Cor. 12:13).

Because you are sons, God sent the Spirit of his Son into our hearts, the Spirit who calls out, "*Abba*, Father." So you are no longer a slave, but a son; and since you are a son, God has made you also an heir (Gal. 4:6-7).

When God saved us, He gave us the gift of the Holy Spirit. The Holy Spirit is God's permanent presence in our lives. He is with us and in us. The Lord is always with us to fight the battle and defeat Goliath. The salvation work of the Holy Spirit is described in several ways in the New Testament: The Spirit baptizes us into the Body of Christ, He indwells us, He seals our salvation, He adopts us into God's family, and He causes us to be born again. Each of these ministries complements the fact that the Holy Spirit has given us a new relationship with God and that He forever lives inside of us.

We never have to face Goliath alone, because the Holy Spirit is always present with us. In his Gospel, Luke describes how Jesus prepared His disciples for spiritual conflict. Like us, these men faced their own Goliaths. The promise Jesus made to them can be claimed by every man of God: "When you are brought before synagogues, rulers and authorities, do not worry about how you will defend yourselves or what you will say, for the Holy Spirit will teach you at that time what you should say" (Luke 12:11-12). Because of salvation, the Holy Spirit is our helper, and He is both with us and in us to empower us. He gives us courage, wisdom and victory when we face Goliath. Once again, the truest thing about us is what God says is true.

The truth of salvation is understood in terms of the work of Christ, the gift of the Holy Spirit and, lastly, in terms of our new identity in Christ. Every man comes into this world with a spiritual identity. We are dead in sin, spiritually identified with our first ancestor—Adam. When we receive God's salvation in Jesus Christ, we receive a new spiritual identity. We are now identified with Christ. Paul explains this concept of identity:

> Nevertheless, death reigned from the time of Adam to the time of Moses, even over those who did not sin by breaking a command, as did Adam, who was a pattern of the one to come.
>
> But the gift is not like the trespass. For if the many died by the trespass of the one man, how much more did God's grace and the gift that came by the grace of the one man, Jesus Christ, overflow to the many! Again, the gift of God is not like the result of the one man's sin: The judgment followed one sin and brought condemnation, but the gift followed many trespasses and brought justification. For if, by the trespass of the one man, death reigned through that one man, how much more will those who receive God's abundant provision of grace and of the gift of righteousness reign in life through the one man, Jesus Christ.
>
> Consequently, just as the result of one trespass was condemnation for all men, so also the result of one act of righteousness was justification that brings life for all men. For just as through the disobedience of the one man the many were made sinners, so also through the obedience of the one man the many will be made righteous.
>
> The law was added so that the trespass might increase. But where sin increased, grace increased all the more, so that, just as sin reigned in death, so also grace might reign through righteousness to bring eternal life through Jesus Christ our Lord (Rom. 5:14-21).

Every man begins with a spiritual identity in Adam. When a man repents and receives Jesus Christ into his life, he receives a new identity in Christ. In Adam, there is sin and death. In Christ, there is righteousness, grace and eternal life. If you are a believer in Jesus, then you are righteous, you are covered by God's grace, and you have eternal life. The truest thing about you is what God says is true.

I recently returned from a men's mission trip to Haiti. Part of the trip was a pastors' conference at which I taught the book of Romans to Haitian pastors. The day after teaching Romans 5, I was having a Coke with my translator, a young man named Jimmy. Jimmy was sharing with me his testimony of coming to know Christ. As he explained how Christ had changed his life, he became excited and repeatedly said, "I am no longer in Adam, I am in Christ! I am no longer in Adam, I am in Christ!" Even though he was a young Christian, he understood the biblical truth of his new identity.

The truth of our new identity gives us a basis to face Goliath with confidence. We are new men in Christ—and as new men, we can claim our gospel position and win the battle. Our new identity in Christ means that we have died with Christ and have been raised up with Christ:

> If we have been united with him like this in his death, we will certainly also be united with him in his resurrection. For we know that our old self was crucified with him so that the body of sin might be done away with, that we should no longer be slaves to sin—because anyone who has died has been freed from sin. Now if we died with Christ, we believe that we will also live with him (Rom. 6:5-8).

We died to our old way of life. We died to the control of sin. We died to living life separate from God. We have been freed from sin's control, and now we have Christ's resurrection life. The truest thing about us is what God says is true. Every man can claim his God-given identity, face Goliath and win the battle. With resurrection boldness and resurrection authority, we can resist temptation and claim our rights as children of God.

Our new identity in Christ includes identification with Christ's death, identification with Christ's resurrection, and identification with Christ's ascension and seating. Paul speaks of this final identification in his letter to the Ephesians:

That power is like the working of his mighty strength, which he exerted in Christ when he raised him from the dead and seated him at his right hand in the heavenly realms, far above all rule and authority, power and dominion, and every title that can be given, not only in the present age but also in the one to come. And God placed all things under his feet and appointed him to be head over everything for the church, which is his body, the fullness of him who fills everything in every way.

As for you, you were dead in your transgressions and sins, in which you used to live when you followed the ways of this world and of the ruler of the kingdom of the air, the spirit who is now at work in those who are disobedient. All of us also lived among them at one time, gratifying the cravings of our sinful nature and following its desires and thoughts. Like the rest, we were by nature objects of wrath. But because of his great love for us, God, who is rich in mercy, made us alive with Christ even when we were dead in transgressions—it is by grace you have been saved. And God raised us up with Christ and seated us with him in the heavenly realms in Christ Jesus (Eph. 1:19–2:6).

God raised Jesus from the dead and seated Him at His right hand. The seating of Jesus Christ is to a place of absolute authority over all creation. He is the Head of the Church and the supreme ruler of angels, demons, men and creatures. Even though we were dead in our sins, God made us alive with Christ. We have been raised up with Christ and seated with Him in the heavenly realms. Our spiritual position is one of complete identification with Christ. We have died with Christ, we have been raised up with Christ, and we are now seated with Christ.

Think about this for a moment: Where is Jesus seated? What authority does Jesus have in His exalted and seated position? What is our identity in Christ? Because we have been seated with Christ, we have Christ's spiritual authority—authority to defeat Goliath, authority to rebuke the devil, authority to resist sin, and authority to win the spiritual battle. We have the authority of Jesus Christ because we are seated with Christ. The truest thing about us is what God says is true!

The good news of the gospel gives us the truth that sets us free and empowers us to face Goliath. Because of the gospel, victory in Christ is the birthright of every godly man. Jesus said, "You will know the truth, and the truth will set you free" (John 8:32).

Discussion

See It
Read 1 Samuel 17:45-47.

- When David faced Goliath, what inspired his confidence of victory?

- In light of Goliath's size and intimidation, what did David understand that gave him this confidence of faith?

Discuss It
- Why do you think it is vital for a man to truly know God and His promises of victory if he is ever going to defeat his Goliaths?

- The hope of victory for every man is the gospel of Jesus Christ. Look up the following verses and discuss the gospel truths that can give men hope in facing their Goliaths: Titus 3:4-7; Ephesians 2:1-10; Colossians 2:8-15; 1 Corinthians 15:1-4,50-58; Romans 8:28-39.

- The power of Goliath is to intimidate us and get us to believe a lie. Jesus said that the truth sets us free. What gospel truths do men need to believe in order to walk in freedom?

Do It
- In this chapter, I define the gospel in terms of (1) the work of Christ, (2) the gift of the Holy Spirit, and (3) our identification with Christ. Which of these truths do you most

need to understand and appropriate in order to defeat your Goliaths?

- Which gospel truths are you going to meditate on, believe and obey in your fight against your Goliaths?

9

FACING GOLIATH IN THE POWER OF THE HOLY SPIRIT

Goliath is a bully. He taunts, he deceives, he attacks, and his mission is to destroy us. Whatever Goliath we may be facing, his purpose is to bring destruction into our life. God calls His men to be strong in the Lord, to acknowledge that the battle belongs to the Lord, and to experience His resources for victory. Scripture is emphatic in this truth: We fight and defeat Goliath when we face him in the power of the Holy Spirit.

First Samuel 17:37-40 reveals a very telling truth about David's confidence in his ability to defeat Goliath:

> Saul said to David, "Go, and the LORD be with you."
>
> Then Saul dressed David in his own tunic. He put a coat of armor on him and a bronze helmet on his head. David fastened on his sword over the tunic and tried walking around, because he was not used to them.
>
> "I cannot go in these," he said to Saul, "because I am not used to them." So he took them off. Then he took his staff in his hand, chose five smooth stones from the stream, put them in the pouch of his shepherd's bag and, with his sling in his hand, approached the Philistine.

David was appalled that Goliath would taunt the armies of the living God. He volunteered to go into the Valley of Elah and fight the giant. Even though he was a youth, David was the only man to step up to the challenge. Looking at David and then looking at Goliath, Saul must have seen David like a high school wrestler entering the Octagon to fight the UFC heavyweight champion. Desperate for David to succeed, Saul came up with a plan. He reasoned that if David had armor and a sword, he might have a chance at victory. Maybe Saul remembered past battles in which these weapons had won him victory. Maybe Saul thought that God would be willing to use these "offerings" as a sacrifice for success. Saul's armor represented the best Saul had to offer—the best of human training, skill and power. Lending this armor to David was equivalent to saying, "When I trust in myself, this is the best I come up with."

But Saul's armor didn't fit the man of God, and David rejected it. He took off the armor of Saul and picked up his slingshot and his shepherd's staff. These were the weapons David had used to fight the lion and the bear, and these were the weapons God had been pleased to use in manifesting His victory. David's confidence was in God, not in himself:

> David said to the Philistine, "You come against me with sword and spear and javelin, but I come against you in the name of the LORD Almighty, the God of the armies of Israel, whom you have defied. This day the LORD will hand you over to me, and I'll strike you down and cut off your head. Today I will give the carcasses of the Philistine army to the birds of the air and the beasts of the earth, and the whole world will know that there is a God in Israel. All those gathered here will know that it is not by sword or spear that the LORD saves; for the battle is the LORD's, and he will give all of you into our hands" (1 Sam. 17:45-47).

David rejected the flesh and put his hope in the power of the Holy Spirit. This is the key for every man who would face and defeat his Goliath. The prophet Jeremiah declares:

> This is what the LORD says: "Cursed is the one who trusts in man, who depends on flesh for his strength and whose

heart turns away from the LORD. He will be like a bush in the wastelands; he will not see prosperity when it comes. He will dwell in the parched places of the desert, in a salt land where no one lives. But blessed is the man who trusts in the LORD, whose confidence is in him. He will be like a tree planted by the water that sends out its roots by the stream. It does not fear when heat comes; its leaves are always green. It has no worries in a year of drought and never fails to bear fruit" (Jer. 17:5-8).

We either trust in ourselves or we trust in God. We either live in the flesh or we live in the Spirit. The apostle Paul exhorts:

But I say, walk by the Spirit, and you will not carry out the desire of the flesh. For the flesh sets its desire against the Spirit, and the Spirit against the flesh; for these are in opposition to one another, so that you may not do the things that you please. But if you are led by the Spirit, you are not under the Law (Gal. 5:16-18, *NASB*).

We can defeat Goliath when we turn from trusting in our flesh and yield ourselves to the Spirit's control.

Several years ago, I was finishing up a men's Bible study that I was leading at a local restaurant. As all the guys were standing up to leave, a young man came up to me and asked if we were Christians. I told him we were, and that we met every week for breakfast and Bible study. He asked for my help and began to tell me his story. He related some tough times in his marriage and shared his feeling that his life was unraveling around him. As he spoke, I noticed that his whole body seemed to be tense and under tremendous stress.

I asked him to hold out his hand, and when he did, I put a quarter in it. I said, "Now make a fist and try not to let me open your hand." Like a vice grip, he squeezed his fist together. One by one, I pulled back his fingers. Each time I pulled a finger, I could see a grimace of pain on his face. Finally, I had all of his fingers pried open, and I took the quarter out of his hand. I asked him, "How did that feel?"

He quickly replied, "It hurt!"

I then put the quarter back into his hand and said, "Now just keep your hand open." He did, and I picked the quarter up off of his palm. I looked him in the eye and asked him, "How did that feel? Did it hurt?"

Of course he said no.

I then explained that God was trying to get his attention. God wanted to draw him into a personal relationship with Jesus Christ—but he would need to surrender his whole life to Christ. Because he was holding on to his life, he was experiencing pain—like the pain he felt when I pried his fingers loose to grab the quarter. I said to him, "You can hold on to your life, trust in yourself, and try to solve your own problems"—here I clenched my fist—"or you can surrender your life to Christ and give Him everything—the good, the bad and the ugly"—and I extended my open palm.

The key to living in the power of the Holy Spirit is to acknowledge that we cannot do it on our own and to fully surrender to Jesus Christ. Paul put it this way:

> But I see a different law in the members of my body, waging war against the law of my mind and making me a prisoner of the law of sin which is in my members. Wretched man that I am! Who will set me free from the body of this death? Thanks be to God through Jesus Christ our Lord! So then, on the one hand I myself with my mind am serving the law of God, but on the other, with my flesh the law of sin.
>
> Therefore there is now no condemnation for those who are in Christ Jesus. For the law of the Spirit of life in Christ Jesus has set you free from the law of sin and of death. For what the Law could not do, weak as it was through the flesh, God did: sending His own Son in the likeness of sinful flesh and as an offering for sin, He condemned sin in the flesh, so that the requirement of the Law might be ful-

filled in us, who do not walk according to the flesh but according to the Spirit (Rom. 7:23–8:4, *NASB*).

Every man struggles with Goliath, because every man has an external enemy—the devil—and every man has an internal enemy—the flesh. The flesh rebels against God and asserts self on the throne. The flesh can be religious or it can be pagan, but either way it does not submit to God, nor does it honor Jesus Christ. To defeat Goliath in the power of the Holy Spirit, we must dethrone the flesh. We must choose to surrender to the Holy Spirit and ask Jesus to empower us and live His resurrection life through us.

In the movie *The Rundown,* starring Dwayne "The Rock" Johnson, a bounty hunter named Beck (played by the Rock) continually faces situations where people have to make choices. At one point he confronts the quarterback of a Super Bowl champion team who had defaulted on a bet, and Beck asks the man to put up his Super Bowl ring as collateral. Beck says, "Option A, you give me the ring; or option B, I make you give me the ring." Option A is the easy way, and option B is the hard way. Paul, like Beck, says we have option A—surrender to the Holy Spirit—or we have option B—live in the flesh. We defeat Goliath when we live in the power of the Holy Spirit. It is a choice—a choice to surrender our lives to the Holy Spirit's control and to ask Him to fill and empower us.

When we are surrendered to the Holy Spirit and filled with His power, we are living a spiritual life. Being "spiritual" is one of three types of existence the Bible describes. In his first letter to the Corinthians, Paul gives us insight into how men can either receive or reject the Holy Spirit's work:

> But God has revealed it to us by his Spirit.
> The Spirit searches all things, even the deep things of God. For who among men knows the thoughts of a man except the man's spirit within him? In the same way no one knows the thoughts of God except the Spirit of God. We have not received the spirit of the world but the Spirit who is from God, that we may understand what God has

freely given us. This is what we speak, not in words taught us by human wisdom but in words taught by the Spirit, expressing spiritual truths in spiritual words. *The man without the Spirit* does not accept the things that come from the Spirit of God, for they are foolishness to him, and he cannot understand them, because they are spiritually discerned. *The spiritual man* makes judgments about all things, but he himself is not subject to any man's judgment: "For who has known the mind of the Lord that he may instruct him?" But we have the mind of Christ.

Brothers, I could not address you as *spiritual* but as *worldly*—mere infants in Christ. I gave you milk, not solid food, for you were not yet ready for it. Indeed, you are still not ready. You are still *worldly*. For since there is jealousy and quarreling among you, are you not *worldly*? Are you not acting like mere men? (1 Cor. 2:10–3:3, emphasis added).

The apostle Paul is describing the work of the Holy Spirit and the different ways people respond to His work. He explains that the Holy Spirit reveals God to us. His job is to lead us into the knowledge of God and to manifest God's presence in our lives. In fact, every aspect of Christian growth, discipleship and service is a fruit of the Holy Spirit's ministry in our lives. He is the only one who can empower us to face and defeat Goliath. Consider this short survey of the Spirit's work:

1. The Spirit regenerates us and causes us to be born again (John 3:1-8).
2. The Spirit leads us into a deeper knowledge of Christ (Eph. 1:16-18).
3. The Spirit guides us into the truth (John 16:13-15).
4. The Spirit empowers us to be witnesses for Christ (Acts 1:8).
5. The Spirit produces His fruit in our lives (Gal. 5:22-23).
6. The Spirit gives us victory over the flesh (Rom. 8:1-17).
7. The Spirit helps us pray (Rom. 8:26-27).
8. The Spirit gives us spiritual gifts (1 Cor. 12).

9. The Spirit sets us free from being selfish (Gal. 5:13-16).
10. The Spirit transforms us to become more like Christ (2 Cor. 3:17-18).
11. The Spirit gives us a heart of worship (Eph. 5:18-20).
12. The Spirit makes us bold to speak God's Word (Acts 4:31).

The passage we are considering, 1 Corinthians 2:10–3:3, describes three kinds of responses to the Spirit's work. They are (1) the man without the Spirit, (2) the spiritual man, and (3) the worldly man. The man without the Spirit is the non-believer. He is the man who rejects the gospel and finds the things of God to be foolish. The spiritual man is the man who has the Holy Spirit in his life and is walking in the Spirit's power. He is the believer who has fully surrendered to Christ and is living a Spirit-filled life. The third type of response to the Spirit is the worldly man. This man is a believer who has received the Spirit—but instead of living a Spirit-filled life, this man is living a carnal, self-centered, worldly life. The worldly man may have been a Christian for some time, but he has failed to grow into maturity in Christ; he continues to live like a spiritual baby.

When my son was about 10 months old, my wife and I took him with us to a nice restaurant. As we enjoyed our meal, he voraciously ate several jars of baby food. He especially liked the green beans. In the dim light, I thought I could see that he had spilled green beans on his bib. As I began to examine the mess, I saw more green beans on the seat of his high chair and all over his legs. I thought, *There are more green beans on him than in the jars I fed him!* Because of the dim lighting, I couldn't see very well, so I bent down to take a closer look—and as I did, I was assaulted by an all-too-familiar smell. Those weren't green beans! My son had had a blow-out to rival Mount St. Helens! Poop was running all down his legs and even dropping onto the restaurant floor. With the care of someone dealing with toxic waste, I picked my son up, carried him at arm's length, and quickly made my way to the bathroom. With every step—*plop plop plop*—poop dropped out of his diapers onto the floor.

When I got to the bathroom, I cleaned him up, changed his diapers, and put a new outfit on him—and that's the end of the story!

Every parent has had a similar experience. Babies poop their diapers and need to be changed. However, if I related the same story, but explained that my son was 18 years old and was still pooping his diapers, you would know that something was wrong. It's okay to act like a baby when you are a baby; it's not okay when you should have grown up and matured.

In 1 Corinthians 3:1-3, Paul is rebuking the worldly man for being immature. Even though he should be spiritual—living a Spirit-controlled life—he is acting like a spiritual baby and being worldly. The writer of Hebrews offers a similar rebuke:

> In fact, though by this time you ought to be teachers, you need someone to teach you the elementary truths of God's word all over again. You need milk, not solid food! Anyone who lives on milk, being still an infant, is not acquainted with the teaching about righteousness. But solid food is for the mature, who by constant use have trained themselves to distinguish good from evil (Heb. 5:12-14).

The worldly man ought to be feeding on God's Word and experiencing the Spirit's work, but instead he is living a carnal life, acting like a spiritual baby, and looking just like the world.

Paul says there are three ways to respond to the Spirit: (1) reject Him and be an unbeliever; (2) receive Him and obey His leading as a spiritual man; or (3) receive Him, but continue to live with self on the throne of your life. *Every Christian has the Spirit, but not every Christian is filled with the Spirit. The Holy Spirit comes into our lives at salvation—but to be filled with the Spirit, we must surrender to Him and obey Him.*

Suppose I have two glasses of milk, and into each glass I squirt an equal amount of chocolate syrup. The syrup drops down to the bottom of the glasses. I take a spoon and stir the milk in one glass. Pretty soon, the milk turns dark. I take a sip—and guess what? I have created chocolate milk! It looks and tastes different from regular milk. The milk has been influenced and transformed by the syrup. The other glass of milk has the same amount of syrup in it, but the syrup is not changing the milk. The liquid in the glass looks just like milk and tastes just like milk. The syrup has to be stirred in to transform the milk.

Every believer in Jesus Christ has the Holy Spirit; some, however, are spiritual and some are worldly. We can only defeat Goliath when we are living Spirit-filled lives. To be filled with the Spirit means we are led, empowered, directed and guided by the Spirit. He is producing His fruit and manifesting His victory in our lives. *In order to be filled with the Spirit, we need to (1) desire the Spirit's work, (2) yield to the Spirit's control, and (3) ask for the Spirit's help.*

We will never experience more of the Spirit's work in our lives than we desire and seek after. John says this about how we are to receive the Spirit:

> On the last and greatest day of the Feast, Jesus stood and said in a loud voice, "If anyone is thirsty, let him come to me and drink. Whoever believes in me, as the Scripture has said, streams of living water will flow from within him." By this he meant the Spirit, whom those who believed in him were later to receive. Up to that time the Spirit had not been given, since Jesus had not yet been glorified (John 7:37-39).

When we are spiritually thirsty and come to Jesus to drink, He satisfies us with the living water of the Holy Spirit. Drinking of the Spirit is to be an ongoing experience in our lives. We are not filled with the Spirit just one time, but many times. In fact, Paul commands, "Do not get drunk on wine, which leads to debauchery. Instead, be filled with the Spirit" (Eph. 5:18). Grammatically, this command is a present passive imperative. Being filled with the Spirit is to be an ongoing experience. It is an experience that we are to allow ourselves to receive from the Spirit. We are to continually allow the Holy Spirit to fill our lives. We are to regularly drink of the Spirit and experience His living water overflowing from our innermost being.

During hell week of my senior year in high school, the temperature soared into triple digits. My high school football coach was of the old school and did not believe in water breaks. We would practice for three hours, twice a day, with no water. During one of the practices, he called the team together for a huddle. Standing in the back of the group, I noticed a lawn sprinkler with a large puddle of brown water encircling it. Feeling the effects of dehydration and longing for any kind of water, I took off my helmet, crouched down, and dunked my head into the puddle. For a few brief seconds, I drank as much water as I could gulp down!

Thirsty people are desperate people. When we are spiritually thirsty, we are desperate for the living water that the Holy Spirit produces in our lives. We experience the fullness of the Spirit when we come to Jesus, desperately seeking His lordship, presence, empowerment and help. When we come to Jesus and continually drink, He fills us with the Spirit, who satisfies us and overflows our lives.

We experience the fullness of the Spirit when we are thirsty and when we yield to His lordship in our lives. Paul exhorts us:

> And if the Spirit of him who raised Jesus from the dead is living in you, he who raised Christ from the dead will also give life to your mortal bodies through his Spirit, who lives in you. Therefore, brothers, we have an obligation—but it is not to the sinful nature, to live according to it. For if you live according to the sinful nature, you will die; but if by the Spirit you put to death the misdeeds of the body, you will live (Rom. 8:11-13).

According to this passage, we have the Spirit of Him who raised Jesus from the dead living inside of us. God's promise is that we will experience His resurrection life through the indwelling Spirit. Our obligation, therefore, is not to live according to our selfish sinful nature. Instead, we are to live according to the Spirit—to surrender to His control and to put to death the misdeeds of the body. Authentic spiritual life is ours when we yield to the Holy

Spirit. The picture is that we have been in the driver's seat of our car. We have controlled the wheel, the gas and the radio! When we trusted in Christ, He came into our lives through the spiritual indwelling of the Holy Spirit. His desire, though, is not just to be a passenger, but to take our place at the wheel. We need to step into the back seat and let the Spirit be in control of our lives. We must surrender every part of our lives—our minds, our wills, our habits, our relationships, our finances—to Him. When we do, He empowers us to resist sin and live victoriously in Christ.

A third prerequisite to experiencing the power of the Holy Spirit in our lives is to ask for His help. Sounds simple, doesn't it? Especially in light of this promise:

> So I say to you: Ask and it will be given to you; seek and you will find; knock and the door will be opened to you. For everyone who asks receives; he who seeks finds; and to him who knocks, the door will be opened. Which of you fathers, if your son asks for a fish, will give him a snake instead? Or if he asks for an egg, will give him a scorpion? If you then, though you are evil, know how to give good gifts to your children, how much more will your Father in heaven give the Holy Spirit to those who ask him! (Luke 11:9-13).

In this passage, Jesus is teaching on prayer and the promises we can claim in prayer. If we keep asking, it will be given to us; if we keep seeking, we will find; and if we keep knocking, the door will be opened. Jesus then uses a Hebrew form of comparison known as the "how much more" argument. Two scenarios are compared, with the second one being assumed because of the obvious nature of the first. Because we know that human fathers want to give good gifts to their children, how much more do we know that our heavenly Father will give a very good gift—the Holy Spirit—to those who ask Him! God desires to help us and bless us with the Holy Spirit even more than we desire to ask Him. *God is waiting for His men to ask for His help. He promises that when we ask for the help of the Holy Spirit, He will answer.*

It is the Holy Spirit's nature to help us. In John 14–16, Jesus refers to the Holy Spirit by using the Greek word *paraclytos*. This word means "someone called alongside to help, encourage or comfort." That is why different Bible translations use the terms "Helper," "Comforter" and "Counselor." Here is a Sunday school question: "If the Holy Spirit is called the Helper by Jesus, then what does He do?" That's right, He helps! Let's look at one of Jesus' specific statements about the *paraclytos*:

> And I will ask the Father, and he will give you another Counselor to be with you forever—the Spirit of truth. The world cannot accept him, because it neither sees him nor knows him. But you know him, for he lives with you and will be in you (John 14:16-17).

Jesus promised that He would send the Counselor to be with us and to be in us. The Holy Spirit, who is the Spirit of truth, is available to help us 24-7.

God's Word promises that if you are thirsty for a deeper spiritual experience, and you come to Jesus to drink, then the Holy Spirit will overflow your life with His living water. If you surrender to Him, He will empower you with Christ's resurrection life. God also says that He will give the Spirit to anyone who asks Him. What are you waiting for? You can live in Christ's victory and defeat Goliath every day when you turn from the flesh and walk in the Spirit. Remember this assurance given by the apostle Paul:

> So I say, live by the Spirit, and you will not gratify the desires of the sinful nature. For the sinful nature desires what is contrary to the Spirit, and the Spirit what is contrary to the sinful nature. They are in conflict with each other, so that you do not do what you want. But if you are led by the Spirit, you are not under law (Gal. 5:16-18).

The Holy Spirit who indwells you is the same Spirit who empowered David to defeat Goliath. He is the same Spirit who led

Jesus to resist the devil and return from the desert in victory. The Holy Spirit empowers our lives, produces His fruit, and gives us spiritual victory. Come to Him as a thirsty man, surrender to His control, and ask Him to fill your life and lead you in Christ's triumph.

Discussion

See It
Read 1 Samuel 17:38-47.

- When David volunteered to fight Goliath, Saul suited him up in his own armor. David rejected the armor of Saul and instead chose his staff and a few rocks for his slingshot. Why do you think we are incapable of defeating Goliath with human resources?

- David understood that "the battle belongs to the Lord." What do you think it means to trust in the power of the Spirit rather than in your own flesh?

Discuss It
- Look up the following verses and discuss the contrast between trusting in the flesh and trusting in the Spirit: Jeremiah 17:5-8; Romans 7:15–8:11; Galatians 5:16-26.

- For a man to defeat his Goliath, he must reject the flesh and trust in the Lord for victory. What does this look like in a man's thought life, choices, habits and daily commitments?

- To depend on the power of the Holy Spirit in order to defeat Goliath, a man must be living a Spirit-filled life. Look up the following verses and discuss the implications for being a Spirit-filled man: John 7:37-39; Romans 8:12-16; Luke 11:13; Galatians 6:7-8.

Do It

- What do you need to do to follow David's example and take off Saul's armor? How are you going to reject the flesh and trust in the power of the Holy Spirit?

- What proactive action do you need to take to walk in the Spirit?

10

FACING GOLIATH IN THE AUTHORITY OF GOD'S WORD

"This book will change your life. Read it every day and ask God to help you understand it and do what it says." With that admonishment, my brother gave me my first Bible when I was 16 years old. Excited about my newfound faith, my brother bought me a New Testament, in the *Living Bible* translation, and gave it to me as a gift. Over the course of the next year, I read my Bible almost every day—sometimes reading just one chapter and sometimes more. Most of the time, I read it at night before I went to sleep. Sometimes I didn't even remember what I had read, because I was tired or preoccupied. But by the end of my senior year in high school, I had finished reading the New Testament, and I had become convinced of my faith and rooted in my new life in Christ.

That summer, I set myself the goal of reading through the Old Testament before I went off to college. Every day, I read several chapters; and by the end of the summer, I had completed my goal. At the beginning of my freshman year in college, I decided to read the New Testament in the morning and the Old Testament at night. I counted the number of pages in my Bible and calculated that I could read through the New Testament every two months and the Old Testament every six months. So, with a love for Christ and a desire to know God's Word, I set about systematically reading the Bible cover to cover.

Without a doubt, this daily habit of reading God's Word has been the most profound influence on my Christian life. More than any other discipline, the daily intake of Scripture has fueled my faith and strengthened my commitment to Jesus Christ. Paul tells us, "Faith comes by hearing, and hearing by the word of God" (Rom. 10:17, *NKJV*). For the past 41 years, the Word of God has been the basis for my faith.

Every man puts his faith in something. We either trust in the Word of God or we trust in our own feelings and perceptions. David trusted in the Word of God. When confronted with the taunts and challenges of Goliath, all the soldiers in the Israelite army saw the giant, heard his arrogant words, and were paralyzed with fear. David heard the same challenges, he saw the same giant, and he experienced the same feelings of righteous indignation for the name of the Lord. The difference was that David's faith was rooted in what God said was true. David believed that God was bigger than Goliath. David believed that God's promises were truer than Goliath's threats. David's perspective was influenced by the Word of God, not by his human fears or limited understanding.

We don't always get to choose which Goliaths we face, but we do get to choose whether we face our Goliaths with our faith in God's Word or our faith in ourselves. To be a man like David, we need to be convinced that God's Word is true and that it is the sword of the Spirit. We need to know what the Bible says, and we need to be trained in the use of the Spirit's sword.

In the movie *Indiana Jones and the Last Crusade,* Harrison Ford plays the Indiana Jones character, who is in search of the Holy Grail. Sean Connery, playing Indiana's father, helps him in this adventure. Following an old map with ancient warnings, Indiana must pass several tests while navigating through a treacherous cave in order to find the Grail. One of the tests is that he must make "a blind leap of faith." (Remember the discussion of Kierkegaard?) Indiana is standing in a huge cavern on the edge of a seemingly bottomless pit. "Take a blind leap," he says to himself as he sees a picture on the map. The picture is of a man walking across the chasm to the entrance of the cave where the Grail has been hidden. From Indiana's perspective—and from the point of view of the movie audience—what lies in front of him looks like a deep gorge with no connection to the other side. Putting his faith in the map, rather than what his eyes can see, Indiana steps off the cliff. At first it looks like he is headed straight into the cavernous deep, but instead his foot lands on solid rock. The camera angle changes—and in what looks like an optical illusion, a hidden bridge connecting both sides is shown to exist. Indiana is affirmed in taking his step of faith.

Faith is always expressed in action. When David put his faith in the Word of God, he boldly stepped into the Valley of Elah. Likewise, when the Israelite army put their faith in their feelings and personal perceptions, they passively retreated into their own fear. We face Goliath when we trust in the Word of God. Hebrews 4:12 states:

> For the word of God is living and active. Sharper than any double-edged sword, it penetrates even to dividing soul and spirit, joints and marrow; it judges the thoughts and attitudes of the heart.

God's Word is life-giving and life-changing. It has the power to impart faith, increase courage and develop character. When we face Goliath with reliance on the Word of God, we are no longer trusting in our own resources; we are trusting in the supernatural resources of God.

Trusting in the Word of God works not because the power is in our capacity to trust, but because the authority is in the Word of God itself. The apostle Peter explains:

> We did not follow cleverly invented stories when we told you about the power and coming of our Lord Jesus Christ, but we were eyewitnesses of his majesty. For he received honor and glory from God the Father when the voice came to him from the Majestic Glory, saying, "This is my Son, whom I love; with him I am well pleased." We ourselves heard this voice that came from heaven when we were with him on the sacred mountain.
>
> And we have the word of the prophets made more certain, and you will do well to pay attention to it, as to a light

shining in a dark place, until the day dawns and the morning star rises in your hearts. Above all, you must understand that no prophecy of Scripture came about by the prophet's own interpretation. For prophecy never had its origin in the will of man, but men spoke from God as they were carried along by the Holy Spirit (2 Pet. 1:16-21).

In this passage, Peter gives us three reasons why trusting in the Word of God is the most reliable foundation for living and the most potent approach to defeating Goliath. *The first reason is that God's Word has the historical credibility of eyewitness testimony.* Peter says that his belief in and presentation of Jesus Christ is not based upon myths. The term he uses for "cleverly invented stories" is the Greek word *muthos,* which was used to describe the Greek myths about the gods. Jesus is not some mythological character. He is a real person who lived, died and was raised again within history. Peter was an eyewitness to the gospel facts. He saw, heard and experienced the great historical truths that became the foundation for the supernatural message of the gospel. Peter was with Jesus on the Mount of Transfiguration. He heard God speak—he personally witnessed the Father saying, "This is my Son, whom I love; with him I am well pleased." Peter's argument is not that we should believe the Word of God because it fits some mythological interpretation of reality; he says we should believe it because it is true and based on historical fact and eyewitness certainty.

A second reason Peter gives for trusting in the Word of God is its innate authority. Peter describes his experience on the Mount of Transfiguration. Jesus was glorified; the great personalities of the Old Testament, Moses and Elijah, somehow materialized; and God the Father spoke with God the Son. By anyone's evaluation, this was one of the greatest religious experiences of all time. Yet Peter says something very profound in response: "And we have the word of the prophets made more certain, and you will do well to pay attention to it, as to a light shining in a dark place, until the day dawns and the morning star rises in your hearts" (v. 19). We have the word of the prophets made more certain. The question is: Made more certain than what? Peter is saying that the word of the prophets—the Word of God—is more reliable than his own powerful religious experience. If God's Word is more authoritative than the best spiritual experience, how much more is this true about bad experiences! When we are discouraged, defeated and deceived, the Word of God tells us the truth and corrects our perspective. The term Peter uses is *bebahyos*, which means "stable, fast or firm." Peter's argument is that the Word is firmer, more stable and more trustworthy than his own awesome spiritual encounter with Christ. The *King James Version* translates this passage as, "We have also a more sure word of prophecy." The basis for our faith is not just our experience; in fact, the authority is not in our experience, but in the more sure word of prophecy.

Because God's Word has authority, Peter exhorts us to pay attention to it. The Word of God is self-authenticating. It is true because it is the ultimate source of truth. We don't go to something else to verify the Word; the Word is how we verify everything else! Even our religious experiences must be evaluated on the basis of the Word. Just because we feel it or think it, that doesn't make it true. God's Word interprets and validates all that is ultimately true and transformative in the Christian life.

The third reason Peter gives for trusting in the Word is that Scripture did not come to us by means of human interpretation. Scripture is the product of men moved by the Holy Spirit speaking the words of God. This is the doctrine of the verbal-plenary inspiration of Scripture. Paul comments in 2 Timothy 3:16, "All Scripture is God-breathed and is useful for teaching, rebuking, correcting and training in righteousness."

All Scripture is God-breathed, or inspired. God literally breathed out His Word into the hearts and minds of the human authors, and they wrote down His Word as the Holy Spirit led and guided them. The upshot of all of this is not merely to inform us on the theology of Scripture, but to transform us into men who face Goliath in the authority of God's Word. Facing Goliath is inevitable, but we get to choose whether we believe his lies or trust in and obey the Word of God. To be men like David, who confidently face

Goliath knowing that the battle is the Lord's, we need to take up "the sword of the Spirit, which is the word of God" (Eph. 6:17).

We fight Goliath with the weapon of God's Word. The movie *Gladiator* stars Russell Crowe in the role of General Maximus, who is betrayed at the beginning of the film. The Roman soldier charged with executing Maximus falters in his ability to take his sword from its sheath. Looking him in the eye, Maximus says, "The frost, sometimes it makes the blade stick." He then kills the soldier and makes his escape. Maximus demonstrates knowledge of the sword and his great skill in using it. God's men need to know the Word and demonstrate skill in using it. We need to know the teachings of the Word of God and know how to be self-feeders in it. We also need to know how to apply Scripture to our lives and use it as a weapon against the temptations, deceptions and accusations of Goliath.

In order to know the Word of God, we have to get it into our lives. Basically, there are five ways we internalize Scripture so that it changes us from the inside out. *The first way to get God's Word into our lives is to hear it.* Remember Paul's words: "Faith comes by hearing, and hearing by the word of God" (Rom. 10:17, *NKJV*). We hear God's Word through sermons, Bible studies, podcasts, radio programs, and speaking it to one another. I have a radio program titled "Truth that Changes Lives." This program, which airs edited versions of my Sunday sermons, is heard all over the world through shortwave radio. My prayer is that every day, someone somewhere will hear the Word of God, believe the gospel and be saved. God's Word has the power to change lives; as we listen to it, we are strengthened and equipped to fight the spiritual battle.

Several years ago, back when cassette tapes were the latest technology, our entire church purchased the New Testament on cassette. We committed ourselves as a congregation to listen through the New Testament over a three-month period. When we hear the Word, it speaks truth into our lives. Every godly man should have a regular intake of hearing God's Word, whether it is through weekly worship attendance, listening to podcasts on our iPhones, hearing the Bible on CD while driving, or maintaining a steady diet of Christian radio. One of the ways we get God's Word into our lives is by hearing it.

A second way to get God's Word into our lives is to read it. In the book of Revelation, John writes, "Blessed is the one who reads the words of this prophecy, and blessed are those who hear it and take to heart what is written in it, because the time is near" (Rev. 1:3). I shared with you my story of reading through the Old and New Testaments as a young believer. That practice has stayed with me, and I daily set aside time for reading Scripture. Sometimes I start at the beginning of the Old or New Testament and read through to the end. Other times I pick a book or a section. I regularly read through the books of Deuteronomy, Psalms and Isaiah, because they were the books that Jesus quoted from more than any others. I also regularly read through the Gospels, because I love the actual words of Jesus. As well, I frequently read through Romans, because it explains the truth of the gospel more clearly than any other book.

The key to all of this is consistency. Start small. Embrace a Bill Murray (*What About Bob?*) theology: "Baby steps, baby steps." Better to read 10 minutes every day on an ongoing basis than to have grandiose dreams and quit after a few days. Some practical advice is to pick a place where you are going to do your Bible reading, pick a time when you are going to do it, and pick a section of the Bible where you are going to start. Once you have those commitments in place, work the plan.

A third way to get God's Word into our lives is through study. Bible study involves asking questions and writing things down. It means that we seek to accurately interpret what we have read by asking ourselves: "What did this mean to the original audience when they received it from the original author? What does God want every generation of Christians to understand from this passage? What is God saying to me personally?" The answers to these questions take work; that's why it is called "study." Paul challenges his disciple, Timothy:

> Do your best to present yourself to God as one approved,
> a workman who does not need to be ashamed and who
> correctly handles the word of truth (2 Tim. 2:15).

Handling the Word of truth accurately takes work, but the fruit is the knowledge of God and His will for our lives. I was a terrible student in college. I don't mean I was dumb; I mean I was undisciplined, didn't go to class and didn't study. Some people graduate *Cum Laude* but I graduated "Thank You, Laude!" This history makes me sympathetic to all the excuses my students give me in the classes I teach at Biola University. But it also has led me to require that students attend class each week, turn in homework each week, and take immediate feedback quizzes each week. My goal is to provide some accountability to help students study. We retain more when we study than when we just casually engage. Some people think that if they just own a Bible, it will somehow wear off on them through osmosis. Others hope against hope that if they sleep with the Bible under their pillow, the truth will magically transfer into their heads and change their lives. No way, José! We must study the Word if we aspire to handle it correctly.

A fourth way to get God's Word into our lives is to memorize it. I know, I know, I have heard it before: "But, J. P., I have a mental block; I just can't memorize." Actually, we all memorize things all the time—useless factoids from school, phone numbers, song lyrics and technical information—truth be told, we memorize a lot of information. This may not translate to the written form, but if you were here with me right now, I would rattle off some of the stupid stuff I have memorized, like: "I am an acne pimple, as lonely as can be; don't cry pimple, I'll keep you company." I remember that from a Clearasil commercial from the 1960s. "When two parallel lines are intersected by a transversal, alternate interior angles are equal." That was from high school geometry in 1971. How about this one—again, this is from the top of my head: "So, I tell them I'm a pro jock, and who do you think they give me? The Dalai Lama, himself. Twelfth son of the Lama; the flowing robes, the grace, bald . . . striking." That's right, Bill Murray in *Caddyshack* from 1980.

What's my point? Somehow I have committed a lot of information—much of it useless—to memory, some of it on purpose and some of it just by repeated exposure. Barring some learning disability, we can all memorize Scripture. The question is, will we do what it takes to memorize God's Word? At the end of His 40 days in the wilderness, Jesus responded to temptation by quoting Scripture back to the devil (see Matt. 4:1-11). The verses He quoted were spot on in defeating the devil's attack. Before Jesus could wield these verses in battle, He first had to internalize and memorize them. Because He had the Word abiding in Him, He was able to use it in defeating Goliath. We get God's Word into our lives by memorizing it. For the godly man seeking to win the spiritual battle, his intake of Scripture should include memorizing God's Word.

A fifth way to get God's Word into our lives is to meditate on it. Meditation is the practice of thinking deeply about Scripture. We review a passage in our mind, we break it down phrase by phrase, and we repeat it back to God. Meditation is the strongest form of reflection on Scripture. God gave Joshua this charge: "Do not let this Book of the Law depart from your mouth; meditate on it day and night, so that you may be careful to do everything written in it. Then you will be prosperous and successful" (Josh. 1:8). God promises success and prosperity to the man who will meditate on His Law and do all that is written in it. When we meditate on Scripture, we align our thoughts, our emotions, our attitudes and our wills with the Word. The psalmist encourages us:

> Blessed is the man who does not walk in the counsel of the wicked or stand in the way of sinners or sit in the seat of mockers. But his delight is in the law of the LORD, and on his law he meditates day and night. He is like a tree planted by streams of water, which yields its fruit in season and whose leaf does not wither. Whatever he does prospers (Ps. 1:1-3).

Meditation on Scripture is an integral part of a godly man's arsenal in defending himself against Goliath. The man who is fully equipped with the Word is the man who spends time meditating on God's Law.

"So, J. P., are you telling me that if I discipline myself to get God's Word into my life, then I will automatically defeat Goliath and win my spiritual battles?"

No! You could be the most knowledgeable loser on the planet. Knowing the Bible doesn't guarantee that we are being changed by its truths. It is when we live out the Scripture in the power of the Holy Spirit that its truth sets us free and transforms our lives. Look at it this way: If you owned a large section of land, and you found out that there was oil underneath it, would you drill one hole and put up one rig to pump oil? Would you be satisfied with barely tapping the resources you had discovered? Or would you use multiple derricks to draw out as much oil as possible? You see, the more we seek, the more we find. The more avenues of getting God's Word into our lives we have, the more potential we are creating for God's Word to impact us. Receiving the Word is the necessary prerequisite for practicing it—and it is when we are doers of the Word that we defeat Goliath.

James warns:

Do not merely listen to the word, and so deceive yourselves. Do what it says. Anyone who listens to the word but does not do what it says is like a man who looks at his face in a mirror and, after looking at himself, goes away and immediately forgets what he looks like. But the man who looks intently into the perfect law that gives freedom, and continues to do this, not forgetting what he has heard, but doing it—he will be blessed in what he does (Jas. 1:22-25).

If we merely listen to the Word, we deceive ourselves. It is like being in the front lines of combat with full gear, an assault rifle and a grenade launcher, but never firing a shot. We are fully equipped, but we just stand there as the enemy charges and murders us. The man who knows the Word but does not do what it says gets just as massacred as the man who does not know the Word at all. In facing Goliath, it is action that makes the difference.

When I asked my then-girlfriend's father for the privilege of marrying his daughter, the conversation went quite differently than I expected. I had been dating his daughter for more than four years, I had been a guest in his home numerous times, and we had always gotten along awesomely. I respected and really liked this man. He was a college football coach, and I had played football; he was a Christian, and I was serving in ministry with Campus Crusade for Christ; he was a fun guy and I was a fun guy—you get the picture! So I called him up and scheduled a time to meet him at his home.

I was greeted at the door, and both he and my girlfriend's mother seated themselves on the couch and invited me to sit down. Right away, I could feel the tension. I explained that I loved their daughter and would like their permission to ask her to marry me.

With a serious demeanor, my girlfriend's father looked me straight in the eye. In his Appalachian accent and his coach's posturing, he said, "Well, kid, I know you love her, but it's action. It's action, kid!"

For the next two hours, with sweat dripping down my armpits and soaking my shirt, I sat there as my soon-to-be father-in-law lectured me on the responsibilities of being a husband and the challenges of marriage. It's action. In marriage and in winning the spiritual battle, it is action. We need to be doers of the Word in order to face and defeat Goliath.

David, trusting in the Word of God and ignoring the taunts of Goliath, descended into the Valley of Elah and defeated his giant. We have at our disposal the same weapon that equipped and empowered David for victory. *When a man takes up the sword of the Spirit and uses the Word of God in obedient action, he experiences the Lord's victory.* Regardless of what your eyes can see, the Word of God is truer than anything you feel. Our ultimate Victor, Jesus Christ, has promised that the truth shall set us free. Let's believe it and let's do it!

Discussion

See It
Read 1 Samuel 17:40-50.

- How would you characterize David's attitude as he ran to face Goliath?

- Why do you think David trusted more in God's promise of victory than he did in Goliath's threats of defeat?

Discuss It

- Every man lives by faith; the difference is the object of our faith. Why is God's Word more authoritative than our perceptions as an object of faith?

- Look up the following verses and discuss what they say about the authority and transforming power of God's Word: Psalm 19:7-11; Jeremiah 23:25-29; Isaiah 55:8-11; Matthew 5:17-19; Ephesians 6:17; Hebrews 4:12; 1 Peter 1:23–2:2; 2 Peter 1:16-21.

- When we know the promises of God, and we claim the authority of His Word, how does that empower and equip us to defeat Goliath?

Do It

- According to Matthew 4:1-11, Jesus appealed to Scripture when He was tempted by the devil, and each Scripture He quoted specifically dealt with that particular temptation. Look up the following promises from God's Word and discuss the specific Goliath's they are targeted to defeat: Galatians 5:16; Isaiah 41:10; 1 Corinthians 6:18-20; Ephesians 4:25-32; Colossians 3:1-11, James 4:6-10; Proverbs 3:5-6.

- What promises do you need to believe and claim so that you can defeat Goliath in the authority of God's Word?

- How are you going to abide in God's Word?

11

FACING GOLIATH
IN THE PROVISION
OF PRAYER

Eight years ago, I was at a crossroads in my life. I had been serving
Christ for 26 years as a missionary, associate pastor and senior pastor. At the time, I was the teaching pastor and director of men's
ministry for a large church in Southern California. The founding
pastor had retired, and many people, including the elders, had
asked me if I wanted to step back into a senior pastor role. At first
I was cautious, but after much prayer I felt that God was leading
me into that position. Unbeknownst to me, during the time that
I was growing in my desire for the job, the elders were reevaluating
me and the position—and they were feeling that I was not the can-
didate for the job.

The time drew near for me to tell the elders whether or not I
was going to pursue the senior pastor position. I had served with
them as a fellow elder for six years, and several of them were in an
accountability group with me, so I felt that they knew me—and
they either believed in me or they didn't. I reasoned, *Hey, you know
who I am. Either offer me the job or let's move on to something else, but
there will be no more candidating or evaluating.* In my mind, I put together everything I was going to say at the meeting.

The night before the meeting, I slept restlessly. I kept thinking
and praying about my meeting with the elders. Suddenly, whether
in a dream or vision, I saw in bold bright letters on the ceiling of my
bedroom the words from 1 Peter 5:6: "Humble yourselves, therefore, under God's mighty hand, that he may lift you up in due
time." I was overwhelmed with a sense that I should not go into

that meeting in a power position but, instead, I should submit to whatever process the elders chose and trust God to direct my life.

So that is precisely what I did. Several months later, I was stunned, crushed and blindsided when they told me that I was not the person they were looking for to lead the church. What had gone wrong? I had prayed and surrendered to God, but I got the exact opposite result of what I expected! Now I was crushed in spirit, felt rejected, and was fearful about my future. I was the teaching pastor, preaching every weekend at that point; I had put myself out there for the job; and now they were going to hire someone else to lead the church. How could I continue in my position of influence? Would the next guy see me as a threat and fire me? Given that I felt like God was calling me back into the role of being a senior pastor, was He leading me to apply for the position at another church? All of these thoughts consumed me. I prayed and prayed but felt that my conflicting emotions clouded my ability to hear God speak to me.

As I continued to earnestly seek the Lord in prayer, I invited some trusted prayer warriors to join me. We drove to Forest Home Conference Center, the place where Billy Graham had wrestled with God in prayer and resolved to preach the gospel for the rest of his life. Standing on the very spot where Graham had prayed, our group cried out to God and asked Him to show me His will for my life. We prayed that God would direct me, provide for me, and show me His call. We prayed for clarity, provision, direction and clear leading from the Lord. I began a 10-day period of prayer and fasting, asking God to reveal to me His will for my life.

Soon afterwards, the Lord—through a whole variety of prayers, people, circumstances and miracles—showed me that His will was to start a new church, targeting a new development near our city. I met with the elders to share with them God's direction in my life and to discuss my exit strategy from the church. After the meeting, I had a sense of peace that God was answering His promise to me from 1 Peter 5:6.

Then I got a warning call from the retiring senior pastor; apparently the elders had gotten together, and fear had clouded their reasoning. They feared that I might try to take members of the church with me to start the new church. They feared that this was out of their control and could result in a church split. After several meetings, my heart was broken. Not only was I rejected for the position of senior pastor, but now men with whom I had served were also doubting my character and assuming that I was seeking to split the church. Never in my 26 years of serving Christ had anyone ever accused me of such a thing.

I was stunned, devastated and broken. I cried out to God, *Lord, You are the God of angel armies—protect me; save me! God, You are my only hope. Protect me from those who slander me. Guard my life and my family. Restore to me the joy of my salvation. Lead me in Your path.* I struggled with the Goliath of fear, and prayer was my only hope. On many occasions, I cried out to God all night, asking for His help, His mercy and His truth to set me free.

After many meetings with the elders, we worked out a plan for me to leave the church without incident or fanfare. While continuing to serve in my position of teaching pastor and director of men's ministry, I agreed to delay the launch of the new church for several months. When we began, we held prayer meetings with a nucleus of 16 people who shared our vision for ministry. It has now been a little over 7 years since we started meeting, and prayer continues to be the heart and soul of our church.

I recently returned from a men's mission trip to Haiti, and my prayers were much different than they were 8 years ago. On the ground in Haiti, I stood in front of a water station we helped build; this station provides clean water to thousands of people. On the front of the building, in large letters, is written Crossline Church— the name of the church I founded. As I looked at the water station, I was overwhelmed with emotion: *God, thank You; thank You for Your blessing. It's not about me; it's about You, Your Kingdom, Your plan.*

Eight years ago, I struggled with the Goliath of fear; my consuming questions were, "What am I going to do with my life? What is God's direction for me?" Eight years later, God has answered and fulfilled His promise from 1 Peter 5:6. Through Crossline Church, more than 1,400 people have publicly given their lives to Christ in South Orange County, California. Our church has grown from 16 to around 2,000 worshipers; missionaries have been sent all over the world; thousands of people have been fed and clothed through our "least of these" ministries; an international radio ministry—"Truth that Changes Lives"—broadcasts the gospel around the world every day; and thousands upon thousands of lives in our community and around the world have been transformed by Jesus Christ. It's not about me! It's about Jesus and His plan.

Goliath could have stopped me in my tracks. My only hope and help was prayer. Just as David defeated Goliath in the Valley of Elah, so too God will help every man defeat his Goliath if that man humbles himself and seeks the Lord in prayer. Prayer is a potent weapon, a spiritual discipline, and a way of life to men who walk with God. David was a man who walked with God. Prayer was a constant help and a deciding factor in his victory over Goliath.

David ran to face Goliath with absolute confidence in the Lord's victory:

> David said to the Philistine, "You come against me with sword and spear and javelin, but I come against you in the name of the LORD Almighty, the God of the armies of Israel, whom you have defied. This day the LORD will hand you over to me, and I'll strike you down and cut off your head. Today I will give the carcasses of the Philistine army to the birds of the air and the beasts of the earth, and the whole world will know that there is a God in Israel. All those gathered here will know that it is not by sword or spear that the LORD saves; for the battle is the LORD's, and he will give all of you into our hands." As the Philistine moved closer to attack him, David ran quickly toward the battle line to meet him (1 Sam. 17:45-48).

David expected to defeat Goliath because David had seen God defend him in the past. Shortly before rushing into battle, David had passionately argued with Saul that the God who had delivered him from the lion and the bear would also deliver him from the Philistine (see vv. 34-37). David was a man who walked with the Lord, and spiritual victory was a byproduct of his relationship with God. As a shepherd, David had spent long nights alone with God. He prayed, he meditated, and he sang songs of worship to his Creator. David knew God. He knew the greatness, the power, the love, the mercy and the holiness of God. David knew God because he spent time with Him.

When I was 23 years old, I went to a UCLA football game and met the woman who would become my wife. She was a freshman in college, and I was a brand-new staff member with Campus Crusade for Christ. I was attending the game with a student I had recently met; this student had gone to high school with my future wife, Donna. When he saw Donna, he greeted her with a big hug and said, "Donna, it's so good to see you!"

Then he turned to me and was about to introduce us—but before he could say anything, I stepped up, gave Donna a big hug and said, "Donna, it's so good to see you!"

The next day, at church, I saw Donna again, and with a serious questioning tone, she asked me, "What are you doing here?"

It took awhile for her to become convinced that I was actually a missionary. Needless to say, I didn't wow her with a first impression. Yet here we are after 27 years of marriage, three kids, a lifetime of precious memories and shared stories, and a growing love affair. The more we have spent time together, the more we have gotten to know each other and grown deeper in our mutual love and trust. Deep relationships are built on spending time together.

David spent time with God, knew God and walked with God. When a man walks with God, God is the defender of his life. When a man walks with God, he trusts the Lord, seeks His help and experiences His victory. The book of Psalms reveals that essential to David's walk with God was David's life of prayer. Prayer connects us with God. Prayer aligns our wills with God's will, and it invites God to be the center of our lives. Every godly man who has ever lived has been a man of prayer. Every man who has ever defeated Goliath has done so in the provision of prayer.

Jesus models this dependence on prayer on numerous occasions. In Mark 1, we read that the disciples rose early and couldn't find Jesus anywhere. After going into search mode, they finally discovered Him alone in prayer. Jesus, the Son of God and the perfect man, found it necessary to begin every day in prayer. Matthew 17 describes how Jesus came down from the Mount of Transfiguration and found His disciples seeking to help a father whose son had demonic seizures. Explaining the disciples' inability to bring healing to the boy, Jesus stated that this kind of miracle could only be done through prayer. Jesus also depended on prayer to give Him victory over His own Goliath:

> Then Jesus went with his disciples to a place called Gethsemane, and he said to them, "Sit here while I go over there and pray." He took Peter and the two sons of Zebedee along with him, and he began to be sorrowful and troubled. Then he said to them, "My soul is overwhelmed with sorrow to the point of death. Stay here and keep watch with me."
>
> Going a little farther, he fell with his face to the ground and prayed, "My Father, if it is possible, may this cup be taken from me. Yet not as I will, but as you will."
>
> Then he returned to his disciples and found them sleeping. "Could you men not keep watch with me for one hour?" he asked Peter. "Watch and pray so that you will not fall into temptation. The spirit is willing, but the body is weak."
>
> He went away a second time and prayed, "My Father, if it is not possible for this cup to be taken away unless I drink it, may your will be done."
>
> When he came back, he again found them sleeping, because their eyes were heavy. So he left them and went away once more and prayed the third time, saying the same thing.
>
> Then he returned to the disciples and said to them, "Are you still sleeping and resting? Look, the hour is near,

and the Son of Man is betrayed into the hands of sinners. Rise, let us go! Here comes my betrayer!" (Matt. 26:36-46).

This passage describes the anguish of soul that Jesus experienced prior to going to the cross and dying for our sins. In order to spiritually and emotionally prepare Himself for the battle He was about to fight, Jesus needed to surrender His heart to the Father in prayer: "My Father, if it is not possible for this cup to be taken away unless I drink it, may your will be done" (v. 42). Prayer vitally encouraged, prepared and strengthened Jesus for the battle.

If we are going to step confidently into our own Valley of Elah, we need to be men of prayer. *We face and defeat Goliath when we are armed with the weapon of prayer.* The apostle Paul mentions this weapon in the context of describing the armor of God: "And pray in the Spirit on all occasions with all kinds of prayers and requests. With this in mind, be alert and always keep on praying for all the saints" (Eph. 6:18). When we employ the weapon of prayer, we are like skilled archers firing deadly strikes into Goliath's heart. In the *Lord of the Rings* movie trilogy, a fictional band of warriors seeks to destroy a mythical ring that is the source of enormous evil power. Among this band is an elf named Legolas, played by Orlando Bloom. Legolas is a fearless fighter, whose skill with a bow and arrow makes him a formidable opponent and tremendous ally. Legolas fires his arrows with trained accuracy and time after time emerges victorious in battle. In the same way, a man trained in prayer is a mighty warrior in God's army. When we fire the arrows of prayer at Goliath, he is neutralized in his attempts to take us down.

Let's look again at Ephesians 6:18, which says something critical for every man's understanding of prayer: "And pray in the Spirit on all occasions with all kinds of prayers and requests. With this in mind, be alert and always keep on praying for all the saints." Paul says we are to pray in the Spirit with "all kinds of prayers." Did you know that there are different "kinds" of prayer? The psalms, largely written by David, give us insight into the different kinds of prayers we are to use in our fight against Goliath. For our purposes, I want to highlight four kinds of prayers: (1) prayers of affirmation, (2) prayers of praise and thanksgiving, (3) prayers of confession and repentance, and (4) prayers of requests. When we use all kinds of prayers, we fire our full arsenal of ammunition at the enemy.

Prayers of affirmation are prayers in which we agree with God concerning what He says is true. We repeat back to God His Word, His promises and His truths. Psalm 23 is an example of a prayer of affirmation:

> The LORD is my shepherd, I shall not be in want.
> He makes me lie down in green pastures,
> he leads me beside quiet waters,
> he restores my soul.
> He guides me in paths of righteousness
> for his name's sake.
> Even though I walk
> through the valley of the shadow of death,
> I will fear no evil,
> for you are with me;
> your rod and your staff,
> they comfort me.
> You prepare a table before me
> in the presence of my enemies.
> You anoint my head with oil;
> my cup overflows.
> Surely goodness and love will follow me
> all the days of my life,
> and I will dwell in the house of the LORD forever.

In this psalm, the psalmist speaks truth to himself, to his Goliath and to God. Prayers of affirmation are prayers of truth. The psalmist declares the truth about God; this declaration gives him courage, gives God praise, and gives Goliath warning! In this psalm, God is affirmed as a shepherd, provider and deliverer—as one who blesses and as a rewarder. The psalmist declares his confidence and reliance upon God. This prayer of affirmation gives the one who prays it confidence in trusting God and in resisting the lies of Goliath. In our prayer arsenal, we need to include prayers of affirmation.

Prayers of praise and thanksgiving acknowledge who God is and what He has done. These prayers are also prayers of truth, and they focus on honoring and glorifying God. When we pray these prayers, they take our focus off of ourselves and off of Goliath—and put our focus on the greatness of God. When we see how big God is, then Goliath looks small. An example of this kind of prayer is Psalm 111:

> Praise the LORD. I will extol the LORD with all my heart
> in the council of the upright and in the assembly.
> Great are the works of the LORD;
> they are pondered by all who delight in them.
> Glorious and majestic are his deeds,
> and his righteousness endures forever.
> He has caused his wonders to be remembered;
> the LORD is gracious and compassionate.
> He provides food for those who fear him;
> he remembers his covenant forever.
> He has shown his people the power of his works,
> giving them the lands of other nations.
> The works of his hands are faithful and just;
> all his precepts are trustworthy.
> They are steadfast for ever and ever,
> done in faithfulness and uprightness.
> He provided redemption for his people;
> he ordained his covenant forever—
> holy and awesome is his name.
> The fear of the LORD is the beginning of wisdom;
> all who follow his precepts have good understanding.
> To him belongs eternal praise.

This psalm declares the greatness of God and recounts His attributes and actions. God is majestic, righteous, compassionate, gracious and faithful. He provides food, works wonders, keeps His covenant, and redeems His people. When we pray prayers like this, our hope and trust in God are rejuvenated, and we gain courage to face our Goliaths. Prayers of praise and thanksgiving need to be prayed when we doubt the greatness of God to defeat Goliath. When we pray these prayers, we feed our faith and strengthen our trust in the Lord.

A third kind of prayer that needs to be in our arsenal is the prayer of confession and repentance. Sometimes we struggle with Goliath because we have sinned against the Lord and opened ourselves up to spiritual attack. Whenever we disobey God in word, attitude or action, we need to confess our sins and step back into the light of God's love and forgiveness. John states:

> But if we walk in the light, as he is in the light, we have fellowship with one another, and the blood of Jesus, his Son, purifies us from all sin. If we claim to be without sin, we deceive ourselves and the truth is not in us. If we confess our sins, he is faithful and just and will forgive us our sins and purify us from all unrighteousness (1 John 1:7-9).

Confession is agreeing with God. We agree with God that our sin is sin; we agree with God that Christ died for our sins, and that through His blood we have full atonement; and we agree with God that we should turn from our sin and repent. Confession keeps us walking in the light and prevents us from developing a deceived and darkened heart. When we pray prayers of confession, we are seeking to get our hearts right with God. Confession and repentance keep us walking in the light and ensure that every piece of God's armor is in place. Psalm 32 is an example of David praying this kind of prayer:

> Blessed is he
> whose transgressions are forgiven,
> whose sins are covered.
> Blessed is the man
> whose sin the LORD does not count against him
> and in whose spirit is no deceit.

When I kept silent,
my bones wasted away
through my groaning all day long.
For day and night
your hand was heavy upon me;
my strength was sapped
as in the heat of summer. *Selah*
Then I acknowledged my sin to you
and did not cover up my iniquity.
I said, "I will confess
my transgressions to the LORD"—
and you forgave
the guilt of my sin.

Therefore let everyone who is godly pray to you
while you may be found;
surely when the mighty waters rise,
they will not reach him.
You are my hiding place;
you will protect me from trouble
and surround me with songs of deliverance (vv. 1-7).

When we harbor unconfessed sin, we separate ourselves from God, and we experience the spiritual, emotional and physical effects of sin's destructiveness. In this target-rich environment, Goliath tempts, deceives and accuses. But when we confess our sins, the light of God's forgiveness covers us, and the power of the Holy Spirit heightens our awareness of Goliath's attacks. Whenever you sin—whether by word, attitude or action—use the weapon of prayer, confessing your sins and repenting of your independence from God. This obedient response will keep you in the sphere of His protection.

The last kind of prayer that we are to pray in facing Goliath is the request-oriented prayer. In this kind of prayer, we ask God to work in our lives. We tell Him how we feel and what we need, and we ask Him for His help. Many of the psalms are this kind of prayer.

When we face Goliath, we need to ask God specifically to help us combat our enemy. An example of this kind of prayer is found in Psalm 25:

> To you, O LORD, I lift up my soul;
> in you I trust, O my God.
> Do not let me be put to shame,
> nor let my enemies triumph over me.
> No one whose hope is in you
> will ever be put to shame,
> but they will be put to shame
> who are treacherous without excuse.
>
> Show me your ways, O LORD,
> teach me your paths;
> guide me in your truth and teach me,
> for you are God my Savior,
> and my hope is in you all day long.
> Remember, O LORD, your great mercy and love,
> for they are from of old.
> Remember not the sins of my youth
> and my rebellious ways;
> according to your love remember me,
> for you are good, O LORD. . . .
>
> Turn to me and be gracious to me,
> for I am lonely and afflicted.
> The troubles of my heart have multiplied;
> free me from my anguish.
> Look upon my affliction and my distress
> and take away all my sins.
> See how my enemies have increased
> and how fiercely they hate me!
> Guard my life and rescue me;
> let me not be put to shame,
> for I take refuge in you.

May integrity and uprightness protect me,
because my hope is in you (vv. 1-7,16-21).

David pours out his heart to God and asks for His help. He asks for direction, grace, protection, forgiveness, rescue, and the reminder of God's mercy and love. This is the honest prayer of a man who is facing Goliath. Every man, if he is honest with himself and with God, resonates with this prayer. This is the kind of prayer that God invites us to pray. When we face Goliath, we can pour out our hearts to God, surrender to His will, trust in His grace, and ask for His help.

We face Goliath in the provision of prayer. When we humble ourselves and ask for God's help, He hears and answers, just as Jesus promised:

> Ask and it will be given to you; seek and you will find; knock and the door will be opened to you. For everyone who asks receives; he who seeks finds; and to him who knocks, the door will be opened. Which of you, if his son asks for bread, will give him a stone? Or if he asks for a fish, will give him a snake? If you, then, though you are evil, know how to give good gifts to your children, how much more will your Father in heaven give good gifts to those who ask him! (Matt. 7:7-11).

With all kinds of prayers, we are to ask our heavenly Father to help us face and defeat Goliath. Because He is good and because He is a promise-keeper, we can expect, like David, to walk into the Valley of Elah and slay our giant.

Discussion

See It
Read 1 Samuel 17:45-47.

- David took off the armor of Saul and put his confidence in the Lord to win the battle. Even before he entered the

Valley of Elah, David was spiritually prepared for victory. What do you think contributed to David's courageous faith and his confidence in God's provision to win the battle?

• How do you think David prayed before he stepped into the Valley of Elah?

Discuss It

• One of the reasons David was so well prepared for victory was that he was a man of prayer. Prayers come in different kinds and categories. Read the following prayers of David and discuss (1) what kind of prayer it is, and (2) how the content of the prayer relates to being prepared for spiritual victory:

    ♦   Psalm 23
    ♦   Psalm 111
    ♦   Psalm 32
    ♦   Psalm 25

• How do you think prayer helps a man be courageous in his faith and prepared to face his Goliath?

Do It

• In light of the Goliaths you are facing, what kind(s) of prayers do you need to pray?

• If you could pray a prayer right now that would give you spiritual victory, what would you pray?

12

FACING GOLIATH WITH THE ARMOR OF GOD

I recently watched, probably for the tenth time, the movie *Troy*. You know you have seen a movie many times when you find yourself completing the dialogue before the actors on the screen do! In *Troy*, a lean and mean Brad Pitt plays the part of Achilles. According to the Greek legend, as an infant, Achilles was dipped into the river Styx, held only by his heel. He became invulnerable, except in the spot where his mother had held him—hence the term "Achilles heel." Close to the climax of the film, Achilles is shot by several arrows, but it is the arrow that strikes his heel that renders the death blow. Every man has an Achilles heel. Every man is vulnerable to spiritual attack. To prepare us for battle and provide for spiritual victory, God outfits us with His armor.

We saw earlier that David rejected the armor of Saul and chose instead the armor of God. Equipped with only a slingshot and a shepherd's staff, David stepped into the Valley of Elah and faced Goliath. David's words to his formidable foe revealed where his confidence lay:

> David said to the Philistine, "You come against me with sword and spear and javelin, but I come against you in the name of the LORD Almighty, the God of the armies of Israel, whom you have defied. This day the LORD will hand you over to me, and I'll strike you down and cut off your head. Today I will give the carcasses of the Philistine army to the birds of the air and the beasts of the earth, and the

whole world will know that there is a God in Israel. All those gathered here will know that it is not by sword or spear that the LORD saves; for the battle is the LORD's, and he will give all of you into our hands" (1 Sam. 17:45-47).

David put his trust in God to win the battle. David stood toe to toe with the largest, scariest and fiercest warrior on earth, and without hesitation, he shouted, "The battle is the Lord's!" In New Testament language, David was equipped with and confident in the armor of God.

The apostle Paul describes that armor in his letter to the Ephesians:

Finally, be strong in the Lord and in his mighty power. Put on the full armor of God so that you can take your stand against the devil's schemes. For our struggle is not against flesh and blood, but against the rulers, against the authorities, against the powers of this dark world and against the spiritual forces of evil in the heavenly realms. Therefore put on the full armor of God, so that when the day of evil comes, you may be able to stand your ground, and after you have done everything, to stand. Stand firm then, with the belt of truth buckled around your waist, with the breastplate of righteousness in place, and with your feet fitted with the readiness that comes from the gospel of peace. In addition to all this, take up the shield of faith, with which you can extinguish all the flaming arrows of the evil one. Take the helmet of salvation and the sword of the Spirit, which is the word of God. And pray in the Spirit on all occasions with all kinds of prayers and requests. With this in mind, be alert and always keep on praying for all the saints. Pray also for me, that whenever I open my mouth, words may be given me so that I will fearlessly make known the mystery of the gospel, for which I am an ambassador in chains. Pray that I may declare it fearlessly, as I should (Eph. 6:10-20).

In this text, Paul gives us the nuts and bolts of spiritual warfare and explains God's resources for spiritual victory.

First of all, he says, "Finally, be strong in the Lord and in his mighty power." In other words, as a conclusion to everything else he has written in this letter, Paul exhorts us to be strong in the Lord. This puts a context on how important it is to live in the Lord's strength. *Our only hope in the spiritual battle is God's strength and power.* He is the one who gives us the victory. Whatever Goliath we may be facing, our ultimate hope is found only in Jesus Christ. First Corinthians 15:57 affirms, "But thanks be to God! He gives us the victory through our Lord Jesus Christ."

When I was a young boy, I used to ride my bicycle around our neighborhood. One day I was out riding when I saw three older boys walking towards me. These kids were known as the neighborhood bullies. As I approached them, they fanned out over the street and blocked me from riding past them. Each of them was carrying a BB gun, and they began to taunt me and threaten to shoot me. One of the boys raised his gun and fired. Immediately the pain spread around the site where I had been hit with the BB. I let out a shout and began to cry. It seemed the more I cried, the louder they laughed. I turned my bicycle around and pedaled home, as fast as I could go.

Arriving at my house, I calmed down a bit—and then became angry at how those bullies had shot me with a BB gun. Emboldened, I got back on my bike and found the three bullies. I rode right up to them and, with newfound confidence, told them to never again bother me or try to shoot me with a BB gun. Looking me in the eye, with fear in their voices, each of the bullies promised me that they would never bother me again. Oh, by the way, when I went home, I got my big brother—and he was standing behind me the whole time I was talking to the three bullies. My brother was the toughest guy in the neighborhood, and everyone knew you didn't mess with him. My courage in facing the bullies came from knowing that my big brother was defending me.

Our courage in fighting the spiritual battle comes from knowing that our strength is in the Lord. He is the one who defeats the enemy, and it is in His strength that we have the victory. Paul says, "But thanks be to God, who always leads us in triumphal procession in Christ and through us spreads everywhere the fragrance of the knowledge of him" (2 Cor. 2:14). We defeat our Goliaths when we walk in Christ's triumph. The battle is the Lord's and our victory is in Jesus Christ. Paul's encouragement is to be strong in the Lord and in His mighty power.

Paul also offers a warning: We need the Lord's strength, because our enemy is the devil and his demons. Behind every Goliath we face—doubt, fear, pride, lust or anger—our real enemy is the devil. Peter tells us we must "be self-controlled and alert. Your enemy the devil prowls around like a roaring lion looking for someone to devour" (1 Pet. 5:8). The devil is our real enemy; he is the archetype Goliath that the human Goliath and every spiritual Goliath represent. Paul describes the nature of our conflict this way:

> For our struggle is not against flesh and blood, but against the rulers, against the authorities, against the powers of this dark world and against the spiritual forces of evil in the heavenly realms (Eph. 6:12).

Our battle is against the devil and his demons. It is not against flesh and blood. We are not in a war with our wives, our kids, our boss, our mother-in-law or the IRS! We are in a spiritual struggle with rulers, authorities and powers. This demonic hierarchy is arrayed against us—and at its head is the devil, who has a strategy to take us down! That is why we need the Lord's strength and mighty power to win the battle.

What God provides for every man to give him victory in the battle is the armor of God. Paul twice commands us to put on the full armor of God; this is the key to facing and defeating our Goliath. The model for this teaching is the armor worn by the Roman soldier. Paul wrote the book of Ephesians while under house arrest. He was literally chained to a Roman soldier. He had the opportunity to observe his armor and chose this metaphor to describe the spiritual resources that God gives to every believer. Let's look once more at Paul's description of the armor:

> Stand firm then, with the belt of truth buckled around your waist, with the breastplate of righteousness in place, and with your feet fitted with the readiness that comes from the gospel of peace. In addition to all this, take up the shield of faith, with which you can extinguish all the flaming arrows of the evil one. Take the helmet of salvation . . . (Eph. 6:14-17).

Just as the physical armor protected the Roman soldier, so too God's armor protects every believer from spiritual attack. *The first piece of armor Paul mentions is truth.* Jesus said, "Then you will know the truth, and the truth will set you free" (John 8:32). Truth is to be worn like a belt across our midsection. It protects us from the lies, deceptions and false teaching of the enemy. If you trace back its source, sin begins with a thought in the mind before it becomes a decision of the will and an action of the body. We make bad decisions and act in sinful ways because our thoughts are deceived and we believe lies. God's truth sets us free from the lies of the enemy.

Remember David and Goliath? Goliath looked intimidating and his threats were menacing. Based on his taunts, the men of Israel believed the lie that there was no way to win the battle. As a result, they were paralyzed with fear. David believed the truth of God and confidently stepped into the Valley of Elah to win the fight. God arms every one of His soldiers with the belt of truth. Today, we have the belt of truth available to us to protect us in the battle.

The second piece of armor Paul mentions is righteousness. Righteousness is compared to a breastplate that covers the chest and vital organs. Every believer is covered in the very righteousness of Jesus Christ. We stand before a holy God, perfect and spotless in His righteousness. This is the New Testament doctrine of justification. God, the righteous Judge, has justified us by declaring us righteous in His sight. The following Scriptures bring this wonderful truth of our righteous position to light:

God made him who had no sin to be sin for us, so that in him we might become the righteousness of God (2 Cor. 5:21).

Therefore, since we have been justified through faith, we have peace with God through our Lord Jesus Christ (Rom. 5:1).

But now a righteousness from God, apart from law, has been made known, to which the Law and the Prophets testify. This righteousness from God comes through faith in Jesus Christ to all who believe (Rom. 3:21-22).

But where sin increased, grace increased all the more, so that, just as sin reigned in death, so also grace might reign through righteousness to bring eternal life through Jesus Christ our Lord (Rom. 5:20-21).

On the basis of our faith in Jesus Christ, God has declared us righteous. We have received the righteousness of Christ, and it is the breastplate that protects us from the assaults of the enemy.

The third piece of armor is the gospel. Paul equates the gospel with the shoes or sandals of the Roman soldier. These sandals were unique in the ancient world in that they were made of leather with iron nails or studs on the soles. This made the sandal similar to a modern football or soccer cleat. With this type of footwear, the soldier had an edge in hand-to-hand combat, especially in mud and soft terrain. Paul exhorts believers to have their feet fitted with the readiness that comes from the gospel of peace.

In his letter to the Romans, Paul wrote, "I am not ashamed of the gospel, because it is the power of God for the salvation of everyone who believes: first for the Jew, then for the Gentile" (Rom. 1:16). The gospel is the message of salvation in Christ. It is the gospel that we have believed, and it is the gospel that we have received as a deposit from God. Paul instructed Timothy, "What you heard from me, keep as the pattern of sound teaching, with faith and love in Christ Jesus. Guard the good deposit that was entrusted to you— guard it with the help of the Holy Spirit who lives in us" (2 Tim.

1:13-14). The gospel declares that people can have peace with God when they believe in Jesus Christ. This message is to give us firm footing when we encounter Goliath. No matter what lies he hurls, or what temptations he seeks to allure us with, the gospel reminds us that we have peace with God and that we are sent on a mission to help others find peace with God.

The next piece of armor is faith. Faith is the shield that protects the godly man from the flaming missiles of the enemy. In the opening scene of the movie *Gladiator,* the Roman Legion is at war with the Germanic tribes. General Maximus, played by Russell Crowe, orders, "At my command, unleash hell!" This is the signal for his archers to dip their arrows in flaming liquid and fire them at the enemy. This was the ancient world's version of artillery. These flaming arrows rained down relentlessly on opposing armies. Protecting the Roman soldier from these flaming darts was his shield. Our enemy, the devil, fires his flaming arrows—lies, temptations and accusations—at us. What protects us from these attacks is the shield of faith.

Faith is accepting God's interpretation of reality. It is trusting in what God says is true and acting upon that truth. God has given every believer a measure of faith. Faith is our shield when we face the attacks of our Goliath. Faith accesses what is true—what God declares and promises in His Word—and then translates that truth into confident action. David faced Goliath with confidence because he was convinced that what God said was truer than anything else. God's promises were truer than Goliath's taunts and truer than the human evaluation of the conflict. Faith apprehends the truth of God. Faith is accepting God's interpretation of reality. Faith is a piece of the armor that God has given to every godly man.

The last piece of armor Paul mentions is the helmet of salvation. Salvation is like a helmet that covers the head. As men of God, we have a covering in Jesus Christ that completely secures our salvation. We are saved! Our sins are forgiven, we have been born again, we have a new nature, we have been declared righteous, and we have received the gift of eternal life! When we face Goliath, we need to have the helmet of salvation in place. We must remember that regardless of the enemy's lies or attacks, our eternal relationship with God is secure. In the same way that a helmet protects the head, Christ's salvation covers and protects us.

The resources that God provides both protect us from the enemy and arm us for victory. *In addition to the armor, God gives every believer spiritual weapons that enable us not merely to defend ourselves, but to actually defeat our Goliaths.* Paul describes the offensive weapons available to every follower of Jesus Christ:

> And the sword of the Spirit, which is the word of God. And pray in the Spirit on all occasions with all kinds of prayers and requests. With this in mind, be alert and always keep on praying for all the saints. Pray also for me, that whenever I open my mouth, words may be given me so that I will fearlessly make known the mystery of the gospel, for which I am an ambassador in chains. Pray that I may declare it fearlessly, as I should (Eph. 6:17-20).

In this passage, Paul describes three weapons God has made available to us: (1) the Word of God, (2) prayer, and (3) preaching the gospel. The Word of God is compared to the sword used by the Roman soldier. This was a short sword known as a *machira*. The *machira* was used in close-quarter combat and required the user to be up close and personal with his opponent. In order to use the sword of the Spirit, we must be right in the enemy's face and strike the deathblow with the Word of God. This means that we need to know the Word, internalize the Word and use the Word.

Our example in using the sword of the Spirit is Jesus Himself, who wielded the Word of God when He was tempted by Satan in the wilderness:

> Jesus, full of the Holy Spirit, returned from the Jordan and was led by the Spirit in the desert, where for forty days he was tempted by the devil. He ate nothing during those days, and at the end of them he was hungry.

The devil said to him, "If you are the Son of God, tell this stone to become bread."

Jesus answered, "It is written: 'Man does not live on bread alone.'"

The devil led him up to a high place and showed him in an instant all the kingdoms of the world. And he said to him, "I will give you all their authority and splendor, for it has been given to me, and I can give it to anyone I want to. So if you worship me, it will all be yours."

Jesus answered, "It is written: 'Worship the Lord your God and serve him only.'"

The devil led him to Jerusalem and had him stand on the highest point of the temple. "If you are the Son of God," he said, "throw yourself down from here. For it is written: 'He will command his angels concerning you to guard you carefully; they will lift you up in their hands, so that you will not strike your foot against a stone.'"

Jesus answered, "It says. 'Do not put the Lord your God to the test.'"

When the devil had finished all this tempting, he left him until an opportune time.

Jesus returned to Galilee in the power of the Spirit, and news about him spread through the whole country-side (Luke 4:1-14).

Jesus lived His life in the power of the Holy Spirit. He is the example for every man. Full of the Holy Spirit, we can use the sword of the Spirit, which is the Word of God. Each time Satan threw out a temptation, Jesus deflected it with the Word of God. Jesus' words, "It is written" and "It says," revealed how He had internalized God's Word and used it to neutralize the enemy's attacks. When Goliath lies, accuses and tempts us, we are to follow the example of Jesus and use the sword of the Spirit. This means that we have to discipline ourselves to know the Word, to understand it, and to be ready to use it any time the enemy attacks. Like a professional boxer who knows how to block a punch and deliver a right cross, we need to know how to use God's Word to stop the enemy's assault and strike a blow that will defeat Goliath.

In addition to the Word of God, prayer is a powerful weapon that gives us victory over the enemy. Paul exhorts, "And pray in the Spirit on all occasions with all kinds of prayers and requests. With this in mind, be alert and always keep on praying for all the saints" (Eph. 6:18). Prayer is a like a supernatural smart bomb that we aim right at the heart of our enemy. Paul tells us to pray in the Spirit. The Holy Spirit is the one who energizes, empowers and activates our prayers. With reliance on the Spirit, we are to pray on all occasions. Prayer isn't just the last resort! We are to begin with prayer, continue with prayer, pray on all occasions, and conclude with prayer.

In our praying, we are to pray all kinds of prayers. Prayers of praise, confession, petition, intercession and every other kind of prayer are to be a part of our prayer arsenal that we unleash against the devil and his demons. The book of Psalms records the inspired prayers of David and other psalmists. These prayers can be claimed and spoken back to God in the power of the Holy Spirit.

As we pray with all kinds of prayers, we not only defend ourselves against the enemy's attacks, but we also launch God's offensive weapons straight at Goliath. As I am writing this, I have just come back from a men's prayer gathering. Every Thursday morning, a group of men from my church gathers in my office for prayer. We pray for ourselves, our families and our church— especially for the men of our church. If this were a mixed martial arts fight in the Octagon, then our prayers would be a flurry of knees, kicks, back fists and left hooks pummeling the Goliaths we face.

The last weapon mentioned by Paul in the Ephesians 6 passage is preaching the gospel. Paul says, "Pray also for me, that whenever I open my mouth, words may be given me so that I will fearlessly make known the mystery of the gospel, for which I am an ambassador in chains. Pray that I may declare it fearlessly, as I should" (vv. 19-20). Paul asks for prayer that he would fearlessly proclaim the gospel. When everything is said and done, the real battle is for people's eternal souls. Heaven and hell are ultimate realities for every person. When we preach the gospel, we are literally taking the fight to the enemy. Because of this, we need the empowerment of the Holy Spirit, the armor of God and the covering of prayer when we share Jesus with others. If Paul needed prayer covering for his evangelism, how much more do we?

As I mentioned previously, I recently returned from a men's mission trip to Haiti. In the midst of unbelievable poverty and suffering, God is doing an awesome Kingdom work there. The spiritual openness is palpable; one can literally walk up to a stranger and begin a fruitful conversation about Jesus. With tears in my eyes, I saw 16 men from our church, many of whom had never witnessed to anyone in their lives, become bold and compassionate evangelists for Jesus. These men will never be the same. They experienced the armor of God and the weapons for spiritual victory. God has called His men not just to fight the spiritual battle, but to win it by putting on His armor and using His weapons.

God desires that His men be armed and dangerous. This means that we must "put on" and "take up" the armor and weapons of God. Ephesians 6:10-20 is not only a promise of God's provision, but also a command to violent military action. We are commanded to be strong in the Lord; we are commanded to stand firm; we are commanded to put on the armor of God; we are commanded to take the sword of the Spirit.

In the movie *Black Hawk Down,* there is a scene in which a group of Army Rangers and Delta Force operators return from a firefight in Mogadishu. Tired, depleted and wounded, the soldiers come into the safety of peers and their home base. Without hesitation, one of the Delta Force operators goes to a weapons table and reloads. In awe, a Ranger inquires about what he is doing. The Delta Force soldier simply says that he is gathering equipment to go back to the fight. Sometimes we become weary in the battle, but Goliath is relentless. Our hope is not in just knowing that God has provided His armor and His weapons. Our hope for victory is when we suit up, arm ourselves for the fight, and punch Goliath in the mouth!

Discussion

See It

Read 1 Samuel 17:41-47.

- When David faced Goliath, he was confident in God's victory. Why do you think David understood that "the battle belongs to the Lord"?

- What resources does God give to every Christ-follower to equip them to win the battle?

Discuss It

- Read Ephesians 6:10-20. Who are we fighting, and what has God provided for our victory?

- According to Ephesians 6:14-17, what are the pieces of the armor, what do they represent, and how do they protect us from the enemy's attack?

- What do you think it means to "put on" and "take up" God's armor? What is our part in receiving and applying God's provision?

- God's armor protects us, and God's weapons equip us to attack and defeat the enemy. Read Ephesians 6:17-20. What three weapons does Paul mention in this passage?

Do It

- We are protected from the attacks of Goliath when we put on and take up God's armor. What piece of the armor do you most need today?

- We defeat our Goliaths when we are equipped with and use God's weapons for victory. What challenges are you facing right now that could become victories for the Lord if you choose to deploy His weapons?

- How can you become more skilled in using the sword of the Spirit, which is God's Word? What do you need to do to become more reliant on prayer for spiritual victory? What steps do you need to take to become bolder and more fearless in sharing the gospel?

13

FACING GOLIATH
BY RUNNING TO BATTLE

David stepped into the Valley of Elah convinced of the Lord's victory. He was God's man for God's purpose. Though Goliath raged and sought to intimidate him, David knew that God was bigger. In fact, David knew that he was called to defeat Goliath:

> David said to the Philistine, "You come against me with sword and spear and javelin, but I come against you in the name of the LORD Almighty, the God of the armies of Israel, whom you have defied. This day the LORD will hand you over to me, and I'll strike you down and cut off your head. Today I will give the carcasses of the Philistine army to the birds of the air and the beasts of the earth, and the whole world will know that there is a God in Israel. All those gathered here will know that it is not by sword or spear that the LORD saves; for the battle is the LORD's, and he will give all of you into our hands."
>
> As the Philistine moved closer to attack him, David ran quickly toward the battle line to meet him. Reaching into his bag and taking out a stone, he slung it and struck the Philistine on the forehead. The stone sank into his forehead, and he fell facedown on the ground.
>
> So David triumphed over the Philistine with a sling and a stone; without a sword in his hand he struck down the Philistine and killed him (1 Sam. 17:45-50).

Every time I read this story, my eye is drawn to verse 48: "David ran quickly toward the battle line to meet him." There was no hesitancy, no passivity, no over-analysis—David ran to battle! Oh, that God would give me and all of His men this kind of balls-out courage and faith. I see something in this account of David's proactive faith and obedience that may help us to follow his example: David entered into the Valley of Elah with a sense of mission and purpose.

The men of Israel, frightened by Goliath's taunts, had lost sight of their identity and their God-ordained call. They were soldiers, called to fight, but Goliath had robbed them of their missional purpose. David was a shepherd; but more than that, he was God's man who followed God's purpose for his life. *We face and defeat Goliath when we are living out God's mission and purpose for our lives.* Living passively, by contrast, invites Goliath to kick our butts.

One of the things my high school football coach used to drill into us was to "play to the whistle." His teaching was that if you play to the whistle, you minimize your chances of getting hurt, and you maximize your chances of contributing to the play. This axiom was painfully brought home to me my freshman year in college.

First let me say that the jump from high school football to college football is a huge reality check. You go from being a big fish in a little pond to being a little fish in a big pond. As part of a pre-game practice during my freshman year, we were doing a full scrimmage of offense against defense. Emotions were running high, and the coaches were allowing a lot of physical contact. I played inside linebacker and was significantly smaller than our offensive line. The scrimmage was fully underway when the coach decided to put me in for several plays.

On this one particular play, the offense ran misdirection and the offensive guard on the right side pulled to become the lead blocker for the running back. As the play unfolded, I stepped up toward the line of scrimmage and moved in the direction of the running back, off tackle. Before a hole could open up, our defensive end crashed down and made the tackle. Seeing that the tackle had already been made, I slowed up—even though I hadn't heard the whistle. Our offensive guard was now at full speed, moving toward the pileup. In my peripheral vision I saw him, and

I thought, *He can see that the play is over and isn't going to hit me.* Famous last words!

As I slowed down and stood up, the guard hit me so hard that I thought it killed my whole family. I was sent airborne and immediately saw stars and heard a weird pinging noise. I thought I had partially lost my vision, only to discover that my helmet had been twisted on my head, and I was looking out through my ear hole! The pinging noise was the screw from my facemask that had been broken and was hanging sideways off my helmet. Without a doubt, that was the hardest I have ever been hit. What made it worse was that I wasn't ready when I should have been. I let up and didn't play to the whistle.

When men let up—when they approach life passively or without a godly missional focus—Goliath hits them so hard that sometimes they don't recover. David didn't casually stroll into the Valley of Elah; he ran to the battle line. He was focused, ready, and pursuing the mission to which he had been called. When we live purposefully, we take the fight to the enemy. Rather than waiting around to be picked off, we defeat Goliath when we intentionally seek after God's call on our lives. God has a Kingdom plan and we are a part of it. In fact, we are Kingdom agents advancing His rule. God has a purpose for our lives that is bigger than our wants and needs. When we see who God is and what He is doing in the world, and we understand our part in His plan, then we can run to battle.

Eight years ago, God led me to start a church. At the time, quite honestly, my vision was very shortsighted. The question I was asking was, "What is the next step God wants me to take for my life?" In a very real way, for me, starting the church was primarily about what I was going to do with my life. Back when we were discussing how we are to face Goliath in the provision of prayer, I shared about the profound experience I had in Haiti. Two weeks ago (as of this writing), I returned from my second trip to that country. I went with a group of 16 men from my church to preach the gospel, feed the hungry and serve the Lord. While in Haiti, we visited many of the projects that our church has been involved with for the past three years—since the earthquake.

As I mentioned earlier, one of those projects was helping to develop a water station to provide clean water for the community of Croix Des Bouquets. The water in Haiti is impure, and many people are diseased with cholera. Clean water is a necessary and precious commodity. Through this water station, thousands of people are blessed. Standing in front of the building that houses the water pumps and filtration system, I noticed the writing in huge letters on the wall: Crossline Church. In Haiti, every day, people are coming to get clean water and are being blessed by Crossline Church. Standing in front of that water station, I broke down and cried. God touched my heart and said, *"My plans are bigger than you. It's not about you; it's about Me and My purposes."* Today we will face Goliath, but it's not about us; it is about God and His kingdom purposes.

When David stepped into the Valley of Elah, he knew that there was something going on that was bigger than a fight between two men. It was even bigger than a battle between two countries. It was a spiritual battle between the kingdom of God and the kingdom of darkness. David ran to the battle line because he knew the battle belonged to the Lord. David faced Goliath with a sense of mission and purpose.

God's men are always called to His purposes. You may recall the story of Elijah and the prophets of Baal. This confrontation took place on Mt. Carmel in Northern Israel, just outside of the modern city of Haifa. I have been to Mt. Carmel and stood where Elijah faced his Goliath. Elijah represented the one true God. Ahab, the king of Israel, had deserted God and instituted the worship of Baal in Israel. Elijah was the constant thorn in Ahab's side. Finally, a showdown between Elijah and all the prophets of Baal took place. The outcome was to be a vindication of the true God: Yahweh or Baal. The contest was to be determined by which one answered from heaven with fire to consume an altar and sacrifice. First the prophets of Baal called out to their god—but nothing happened. Then Elijah stepped up to pray to the one true God—the God of Israel:

Then Elijah said to all the people, "Come here to me." They came to him, and he repaired the altar of the LORD, which was in ruins. Elijah took twelve stones, one for each of the tribes descended from Jacob, to whom the word of the LORD had come, saying, "Your name shall be Israel." With the stones he built an altar in the name of the LORD, and he dug a trench around it large enough to hold two seahs of seed. He arranged the wood, cut the bull into pieces and laid it on the wood. Then he said to them, "Fill four large jars with water and pour it on the offering and on the wood."

"Do it again," he said, and they did it again.

"Do it a third time," he ordered, and they did it the third time. The water ran down around the altar and even filled the trench.

At the time of sacrifice, the prophet Elijah stepped forward and prayed: "O LORD, God of Abraham, Isaac and Israel, let it be known today that you are God in Israel and that I am your servant and have done all these things at your command. Answer me, O LORD, answer me, so these people will know that you, O LORD, are God, and that you are turning their hearts back again."

Then the fire of the LORD fell and burned up the sacrifice, the wood, the stones and the soil, and also licked up the water in the trench.

When all the people saw this, they fell prostrate and cried, "The LORD—he is God! The LORD—he is God!" (1 Kings 18:30-39).

Before Elijah could say, "In God's name. Amen," fire came down from heaven and consumed the altar and sacrifice.

God answered by fire. Everyone was in awe and knew that the Lord was God. Elijah ran to battle. He stepped up on Mt. Carmel as God's man, pursuing God's purpose for his life. God wanted all Israel to know that He was God. Elijah's spiritual battle was bigger than Elijah and Ahab. It was bigger than Elijah and the prophets of Baal. It was a battle of the kingdom of God against the kingdom of darkness. Elijah faced his Goliath with a sense of mission and purpose.

The apostle Paul is another example of living with purpose. By anyone's evaluation, Paul was the greatest Christian who ever lived. In Acts 20, we see Paul gathering the elders from the church at Ephesus to give them his farewell address. God had revealed to Paul that His plan was for Paul to go to Jerusalem and then on to Rome. Paul knew that he might not see these men again, and he wanted to encourage them in their work. With heartfelt tenderness and conviction, Paul recounted his ministry in their lives, and their response to the gospel of Christ. In the midst of this address, Paul said the following:

> And now, compelled by the Spirit, I am going to Jerusalem, not knowing what will happen to me there. I only know that in every city the Holy Spirit warns me that prison and hardships are facing me. However, I consider my life worth nothing to me, if only I may finish the race and complete the task the Lord Jesus has given me—the task of testifying to the gospel of God's grace (vv. 22-24).

Paul anticipated the Goliaths of prison and hardship. He knew what it was like to be in the thick of spiritual conflict. Paul also knew that his life was not his own. He knew that life was bigger than his personal comfort and safety. Paul was sold out for God's purposes. He lived with a clear and urgent sense of his mission: to testify to the gospel of God's grace. Because Paul had been transformed by God's grace, and because he knew that he was called to proclaim God's grace, he ran to battle, fully expecting to face and defeat his Goliath.

Of course, the strongest example of running to battle with a sense of mission and purpose is Jesus Christ. Christ went toe to toe with Satan on multiple occasions and defeated him every time. Jesus lived every day with purpose. He knew that His life mattered for something much bigger than His own success or spiritual victory. In John 17, we hear a unique conversation between God the Son and God the Father. Jesus poured out His heart before He went to the cross to make atonement for the sins of the world:

After Jesus said this, he looked toward heaven and prayed: "Father, the time has come. Glorify your Son, that your Son may glorify you. For you granted him authority over all people that he might give eternal life to all those you have given him. Now this is eternal life: that they may know you, the only true God, and Jesus Christ, whom you have sent. I have brought you glory on earth by completing the work you gave me to do. And now, Father, glorify me in your presence with the glory I had with you before the world began (John 17:1-5).

In this prayer, Jesus reveals that everything about His life was for the purpose of glorifying God. Jesus completed the work that God had given Him to do—and in completing that work, He brought God glory. Every day brings new opportunities for us to glorify God. Every relationship, every decision and every pursuit is a means to an end. The end for which we have been called is to bring God glory. Facing Goliath is a means to that end. We win the fight when we run to battle with a sense of mission and purpose.

So what, specifically, is God's purpose for our lives? What is the mission that should drive us, empower us and give us courage to face Goliath? I believe the purpose that ought to orient our lives is the same purpose that empowered every godly man in Scripture. *That purpose is to glorify God by knowing Christ and making Him known through the power of the Holy Spirit.* When a man accepts this mission, his whole life comes into focus, and he is able to put everything into a God-ordained perspective. Facing Goliath becomes part of God's plan; it isn't something to run away from but to run to. Every day becomes a Valley of Elah to step into in the Lord's strength, confident in the Lord's victory. Running to battle motivated by God's missional purpose is so significant that we need to unpack what it means, so that we fully integrate all of our lives around His call.

Our purpose is to glorify God by knowing Christ and making Him known through the power of the Holy Spirit. The glory of God is His manifested presence. The Hebrew term for this concept is *kabod*, and in Greek the word is *doxa*. Both words imply an impression, a manifestation, an appearance, and a remaining mark that is left. God's glory is God showing up, being Himself, doing what He does, and getting the credit. To glorify God is to show off who God is and what God does. We glorify God when people see in us His attributes, His character, His heart and His salvation. More than anyone else, Jesus glorified God in His very being: "For God, who said, 'Let light shine out of darkness,' made his light shine in our hearts to give us the light of the knowledge of the glory of God in the face of Christ" (2 Cor. 4:6). We glorify God when we manifest Jesus to others. In the Sermon on the Mount, Jesus said:

> You are the light of the world. A city on a hill cannot be hidden. Neither do people light a lamp and put it under a bowl. Instead they put it on its stand, and it gives light to everyone in the house. In the same way, let your light shine before men, that they may see your good deeds and praise your Father in heaven (Matt. 5:14-16).

Every family has its quirky idiosyncrasies. In our family, we memorize movie lines and repeat them to one another as commentary on wacky family moments. Come on, you have wacky family moments just like I do! One of the lines we say comes from the Disney movie *Mulan*. Fa Mulan is a young girl who disguises herself as a boy and fights in China's defense against the Mongol hordes. As Mulan is going off to war, she is exhorted to bring honor to the family, and then the characters break out in song: "Please bring honor to us all." In the same way, we will often say to one another in our family, "Please bring honor to us all." What we are saying is, don't bring us shame; instead bring us glory.

Our mission in life is to bring God glory. We are not to do this passively, but proactively: "So whether you eat or drink or whatever you do, do it all for the glory of God" (1 Cor. 10:31). We are to intentionally live life in a way that glorifies God. Goliath is not a peripheral character in the script of our lives but an antagonist who provides an opportunity for us to fulfill our destiny. When we run to battle, we face Goliath to the glory of God.

Our purpose is to glorify God by knowing Christ and making Him known, through the power of the Holy Spirit. Our seeking to know Christ brings God glory. The apostle Paul said that knowing Christ was of surpassing value:

> But whatever was to my profit I now consider loss for the sake of Christ. What is more, I consider everything a loss compared to the surpassing greatness of knowing Christ Jesus my Lord, for whose sake I have lost all things. I consider them rubbish, that I may gain Christ and be found in him, not having a righteousness of my own that comes from the law, but that which is through faith in Christ—the righteousness that comes from God and is by faith. I want to know Christ and the power of his resurrection and the fellowship of sharing in his sufferings, becoming like him in his death, and so, somehow, to attain to the resurrection from the dead. Not that I have already obtained all this, or have already been made perfect, but I press on to take hold of that for which Christ Jesus took hold of me (Phil. 3:7-12).

Paul looked at his life and said that everything in it was rubbish compared to knowing Christ. All the stuff in his resume, all his degrees, his bank account, his 401k, his BMW chariot, his Rolex sundial—everything he could put value on or hope in was nothing compared to Christ. In fact, Paul was a little more graphic than our modern translations let on. The term translated as "rubbish" is the Greek word *skubalon*—which was a euphemism for animal excrement. To use a modern expression, Paul said that whatever we compare with knowing Christ is just a pile of crap. So, while the world and many deceived Christians pursue after crap, Paul tells us to pursue the knowledge of Christ.

When knowing Christ is our aim, we run to battle. We see life as filled with possibilities, challenges and opportunities. Everything is a learning experience that helps us to grow closer to Jesus Christ. That Goliath, which we desperately wish God would take away from our life, may be the very springboard we need in order to attain a deeper knowledge of Christ. We are to run to battle with a sense of mission, motivated by a desire to glorify God by knowing Jesus Christ.

Our purpose is to glorify God by knowing Christ and making Him known, through the power of the Holy Spirit. Making Christ known means living a contagious life as an ambassador of Jesus Christ. Paul wrote to the church at Corinth:

> Therefore, if anyone is in Christ, he is a new creation; the old has gone, the new has come! All this is from God, who reconciled us to himself through Christ and gave us the ministry of reconciliation: that God was reconciling the world to himself in Christ, not counting men's sins against them. And he has committed to us the message of reconciliation. We are therefore Christ's ambassadors, as though God were making his appeal through us. We implore you on Christ's behalf: Be reconciled to God (2 Cor. 5:17-20).

Our lives and our words are to be in congruence as witnesses for Jesus Christ. Sometimes people ask me, "Can I be a witness by my life or do I need to actually share the gospel with people?"

My answer is always the same: "Yes!" It is not an either/or dilemma. We have the privilege of both being an example of Christ to others and speaking the gospel to others.

Somehow I managed to cram four years' worth of college into five-and-a-half years. Right after I graduated, I attended a conference sponsored by Campus Crusade for Christ. The speaker was Campus Crusade's founder and president, Dr. Bill Bright. Dr. Bright was addressing about 1,000 young people on the topic "How to help fulfill the Great Commission." Dr. Bright looked out over the crowd and asked this question: "What is the greatest thing that has ever happened to you?"

Sitting in the audience, I answered the question in my own thoughts: *Coming to know Jesus as my Lord and Savior.*

He then followed up with another question: "What is the greatest thing you could do for someone else?"

Again, in the silence of my mind, I answered, *Help others come to know Christ as their Savior.*

Dr. Bright went on to speak to those at the conference about how we could orient our lives around helping to fulfill the Great Commission. For the last 35 years, that is the mission that has guided my life: to know Christ and to make Him known. When we live our lives in alignment with God's purposes, we run to battle and live with a sense of mission and destiny.

Being a witness for Jesus Christ is really all about following our Master. Jesus promised Peter and Andrew, "Follow me, and I will make you fishers of men" (Matt. 4:19). I've heard it said that "If you ain't fishing, then you ain't following!" In our church, we talk about being contagious for Christ. When you are contagious, you have the real disease—and you infect others. Many claim to be Christians—and may be well versed in Christian doctrine—but there is nothing contagious about their lives. Others may lack apologetic answers and biblical knowledge, but Jesus is overflowing from their lives, and people are influenced for Christ through them.

I have discovered that the more I know Christ, the more I become like Him; and the more I become like Him, the more I am contagious for Him. When we live with a commitment to God's purpose for our lives, we see that it's not just about us. God has a kingdom plan and we are a part of it. Running to battle means that we live with mission and purpose—and if Goliath gets in our way, then we take him out in the Lord's strength. The battle is the Lord's!

Our purpose is to glorify God by knowing Christ and making Him known, through the power of the Holy Spirit. We have already shown that the only way we can face Goliath is through the power of the Holy Spirit. He is the Activator and Helper in the Christian life. We pursue the mission to which God has called us in the power of the Holy Spirit. He enables us to know Christ and to make Him known. When we live in the Spirit's power, He produces His fruit in us to the glory of God. We run to battle in the fullness of the Holy Spirit.

When I was a kid, there was a Kool-Aid style drink called a Fizzy. Fizzies were like Alka-Seltzer tablets, and they came in different flavors; cherry, grape, root beer, and so on. When you dropped a Fizzy into a glass of water, it immediately began to fizz, and the flavor was released. Something about the chemical make-up of the Fizzy tablet caused it to react when it came in contact with water. The Holy Spirit's ministry in our lives is like that Fizzy tablet. When we put our faith in Christ, we receive the Spirit of Christ into our hearts. He permanently indwells every believer—and on contact, He begins to transform us and make us more like Christ. Like a Fizzy, the Holy Spirit releases within us His fruit and the resurrection life of Jesus Christ (see Rom. 8:11; Gal. 5:22-23).

> Now the Lord is the Spirit, and where the Spirit of the Lord is, there is freedom. And we, who with unveiled faces all reflect the Lord's glory, are being transformed into his likeness with ever-increasing glory, which comes from the Lord, who is the Spirit (2 Cor. 3:17-18).

The Holy Spirit transforms us, activates Christ's life within us, and empowers us to glorify Christ. We run to battle when we seek to glorify God by knowing Christ and making Him known, through the power of the Holy Spirit.

There are only three options for every man: (1) Live a passive, wimpy life; (2) live proactively, but seek to fulfill some purpose other than God's plan for your life; (3) live with a sense of mission and purpose, seeking God's will in every area of your life. We run to battle, facing and defeating our Goliaths, when we live life according to God's mission and purpose. Don't be a wimp. Don't be an idolater. Live on purpose and defeat Goliath!

At this point, some of you are fired up and saying, "Give me my helmet! I'll go in." Others are feeling the guilt and shame of failure. Maybe you have tried to follow God and face Goliath, only to be beaten or to give in to sin. You may be asking, "What if I have failed?" or "What if I've fallen?" The answer is: You've got to get back up.

Several years ago, I participated in a sports ministry where we played American football in Eastern Europe and Russia. Using sports as a platform, we preached Christ, spoke in camps and churches, and discipled athletes from the former Soviet Union. On one occasion, we were playing football in the city of Kharkov, Ukraine. There were probably about 10,000 people in attendance, and our opponents were all former professional and Olympic athletes. We were old and out of shape, but we were much better football players than our opponents.

On one of the kickoffs after we had scored a touchdown, the Russians ran the ball back using a wedge formation. I was the last man on the right sideline. My job was to prevent the return man from breaking away down the sideline. With adrenaline pumping, I sprinted down the field and saw in my peripheral vision a Russian blocker coming right toward me. At the same time, I saw the ball carrier move headfirst into the pileup at the wedge. Before I could process all that was happening, my Russian opponent lowered his head and lit me up. It was an awesome block and I was on the receiving end. I was lifted up into the air and landed hard on my back.

To be truthful, my first thought was, *Great, everyone just saw me get the crap kicked out me!* Now, anyone who has ever played football remembers all the up-downs, bear crawls and fumble rolls they practiced over and over again. Instinctively, even though I had been knocked down—hard!—I got up. What happened next was beautiful. While I was getting flattened, the ball carrier broke free from the pileup—and now he was sprinting untouched for the sideline. He must have seen me on the ground and started to run right around me. I didn't know this, because I was knocked down—so I didn't have a strategy in mind as I got up, but the timing was perfect. As I rose from the ground, the runner ran right into me. My getting up put my helmet into his chest—and laid him out in a photo-op form tackle. I got a solo tackle and all I did was get up!

If Goliath has knocked you down, or if you have taken yourself out of the fight, then get up. Just get up! Assume your God-ordained identity, ask for the help of the Holy Spirit, and run to the battle.

Discussion

See It

Read 1 Samuel 17:45-50.

- What do you think was going on in David's mind and heart that led him to actually run to the battle line?

- What do you think ought to motivate the godly man to face his Goliaths?

Discuss It

- David fought Goliath with a sense of mission and purpose. Look up the following biblical examples and discuss the mission and purpose evident in each man of God: 1 Kings 18:30-39; Nehemiah 1:1–2:5; 1 Corinthians 9:19-27.

- God has called every man to run to battle with a sense of mission and purpose. In this chapter I state, "Our purpose is to glorify God by knowing Jesus Christ and making Him known, through the power of the Holy Spirit." What do you think of this purpose statement?

- Discuss how the following Scriptures clarify God's purpose for your life: Philippians 3:7-14; Colossians 1:28-29; 2 Corinthians 3:17-18; 1 Corinthians 10:31; Matthew 5:13-16.

Do It

- Personalizing this chapter and the above Scriptures, what do you believe is God's purpose and mission for your life?

- How are you going to run to battle?

GOD IS LOOKING FOR MEN

The challenge of the Great Commission is to preach the gospel to all creation. This includes young and old, rich and poor, male and female. The love of God is generous enough to encompass the whole world. With all of humanity in mind, God is looking for men who will lead His Church and advance His kingdom. *It has been said that the Church is the hope of the world. I would add that men are the hope of the Church.* This is not a chauvinistic statement—in fact, my wife approved it! The question before every church is, where are the men? Even a cursory reading of Scripture reveals that God is looking for men. Consider the following passages:

> I searched for a man among them who would build up the wall and stand in the gap before Me for the land, so that I would not destroy it; but I found no one (Ezek. 22:30, *NASB*).

> The saying is trustworthy: If anyone aspires to the office of overseer, he desires a noble task (1 Tim. 3:1, *ESV*).

> The things which you have heard from me in the presence of many witnesses, entrust these to faithful men who will be able to teach others also (2 Tim. 2:2, *NASB*).

God is looking for men with humble hearts—men who will sacrifice everything for the cause of Christ, and who will stand in the gap as servant leaders for their families and for Christ's kingdom. Robert Coleman put it this way in his book *Master Plan of Evangelism*:

> It all started by Jesus calling a few men to follow him. . . . His concern was not with programs to reach the multitudes, but with men whom the multitudes would follow. . . . Men were to be His method of winning the world to God.[1]

The Church needs an intentional strategy to reach men, because if you reach a man, you reach his whole family. A changed man will influence a marriage and a family for Christ. A changed family will influence a neighborhood and a community for Christ. A changed community will influence a state and a nation for Christ. A changed nation will help change the world for Christ. *It all begins with a changed man.*

Dick Marcinko, author of the *Rogue Warrior* series and former commander of Seal Team Six, once said, "We don't need any more weak-willed men. What we need are some brass-balled warriors!" Martyred missionary Jim Elliot, in a more biblical fashion, recorded these words in his personal journal:

> We are so utterly ordinary, so commonplace, while we profess to know a Power the Twentieth Century does not reckon with. But we are "harmless" and therefore unharmed. We are spiritual pacifists, non-militants, conscientious objectors in this battle-to-the-death with principalities and powers in high places. Meekness must be had for contact with men, but brass, outspoken boldness is required to take part in the comradeship of the Cross. We are "sideliners"—coaching and criticizing the real wrestlers while content to sit by and leave the enemies of God unchallenged. The world cannot hate us; we are too much like its own. Oh, that God would make us dangerous!

God is looking for dangerous men—men who will put their confidence in Christ and change the world. God is looking for men who will step into the Valley of Elah and run to battle.

Will you be that man?

Note

1. Dr. Robert E. Coleman, *The Master Plan of Evangelism* (Grand Rapids, MI: Revell, 2010), p. 21.

ACKNOWLEDGMENTS

I want to say thank you to my big brother, Bob, for sharing the gospel of Jesus Christ with me. I want to acknowledge the ministry of Campus Crusade for Christ for being the tool that God used to disciple me and equip me for serving Christ. I want to thank the men's ministries of Coast Hills Community Church and Crossline Church for allowing me to field test the principles in this book.

To my friends at Regal Books, I want to thank Kim Bangs and Stan Jantz for their encouragement and guidance. And to all the men I have had the privilege of mentoring, the apostle John put it best: "I have no greater joy than this, to hear of my children walking in the truth" (3 John 1:4, *NASB*).

To contact J. P. Jones, read his blogs, book him as a speaker and order resource materials, visit:

www.pastorjpjones.com

Twitter: @pastorjpjones